Sh[illegible]ops
[illegible]ns

Essays on the Antiques Trade

Amy Gale

Witlings Press

ISBN: 978-0615846989
Library of Congress Control Number: 2013913248

Cover by Jennie Gale after *Bookseller and Author* by Thomas Rowlandson (Yale Center for British Art)
www.jenniegale.com

Printing/Distribution provided through:
Amazon, Inc
www.amazon.com

Published in the United States of America
First Edition August 2013
Witlings Press

To my parents

Contents

Acknowledgements

Many people have contributed to this book. Most of these essays first appeared in *AntiqueWeek*, under the editorship of Connie Swaim and Dave Blower. John Huckans of *Book Source Magazine* provided sensitive feedback. Thanks, also, to Peter Pach of the *Hartford Courant*.

My sister designed the cover based on a drawing in the collection of the Yale Center for British Art. My parents provided invaluable help.

Finally, I would like to acknowledge the dealers. They have taught me much.

People and Places

Early Memories of a Book Fair

AntiqueWeek, June 2, 2008

For antiques collectors, the fall is the start of the show season. Book collectors have a longer wait. Apart from Chicago and Boston—the big autumn shows—it's only after the New Year that things take off. The succession of winter and spring shows culminates in the big one: the New York Antiquarian Book Fair, which is held in April at the Seventh Regiment Armory.

Many years ago I helped out at the fair. I worked as an assistant to a book dealer specializing in women's history and literature. It's a field with strong crossovers to gender theory and labor studies, but that's not what this dealer liked to sell. Instead the focus was on the eighteenth and nineteenth centuries. Memoirs by aristocratic ladies made up a big part of the inventory. Plentiful, too, were the epistolary novels bound in gilt-tooled tan calf.

"Oh yes, one of the lesser fairs" was the breezy dismissal of one picture dealer. Rare books lag in social cachet, associated as the field is with the earnest and introverted.

I have fond memories of those days. In the months leading up to the fair I helped research and edit the catalog. Sometimes I would meet the dealer for lunch, while other times I would go to her apartment, which was across the street from where I worked. The fair is organized by the Antiquarian Booksellers' Association of America, but she never mentioned the organizer. She did not say the "ABAA fair." It was simply "the fair"—as in, "Would you like to help at the fair in April?"

I met the most delightful people. There were the collecting couples. One stands out: the Hogarth Press for him and Virginia Woolf for her. They bought a few things—only a few because there was not much left to acquire—then stayed to chat about *Mrs. Dalloway.* Another favorite was the college president who came back every year to add to his Willa Cather collection. He played in an amateur orchestra. New York was only just emerging as a livable city. It was safer and cleaner, but the day when Times Square would become a family destination had not yet arrived. It was a source of wonder that all this refinement flourished side by side with the squalor.

We also made sales to modest collectors, who would fasten on a suffrage pamphlet for a hundred dollars. That's a lot of money, especially when you add in the sales tax. Often they had to walk around to think it over. Sometimes they came back resolved to buy. After the bills and coins were exactly counted out, I would wrap the item in a clear plastic bag and seal it with an official sale sticker. These transactions tended to be a little solemn, as if something more momentous than buying and selling were going on.

Of course, not all sales were at this emotional pitch. The esoteric and scholarly book world attracts its share of the stupid rich. These people have to spend their money somewhere, and it's no surprise if some end up at a book fair. Thanks to them, we did a thriving business in Victorian gilt-stamped bindings. I remember holding up copies of *Cranford* and *Evelina* for one lady, who asked her husband, "What do you think, dear? Should we take the blue or the red?"

Most dreaded of all were the bores. While the fine arts draw the vacuous, with rare books you get the bores. You could conveniently and with no loss of precision divide them into two groups: men and women. The men talked about Samuel Johnson. The women made silly claims for some deservedly obsolete authoress. The men were obtuse and condescending. The women were easily provoked. They never bought anything.

Evergreens of the trade: that's what these anecdotes are. Some of my memories, though, have a period flavor. It was the 1990s, when all those movie adaptations of the Jane Austen novels were being made. We flogged early—and not so early—editions of *Pride and Prejudice.* They sold quickly. Every few hours I was told to "put another *P & P* in the case."

On one occasion, I sold a set of Jane Austen novels. The dealer was making the rounds, so I was left in charge of the booth. The buyer was a retired Microsoft executive, who wanted a present for his daughter. His attention was fixed by a green clothbound set that was so much prettier, I freely told him, than the leather bindings.

Before paying, he needed to call his wife. This is where things get hazy. Where did he make the call? Could it be that as recently as the last decade millionaire software engineers were using the pay phone? Or perhaps he had one of those bulky phones stashed in his briefcase, which he had to retrieve from the coat check. The one thing he did not do was whip out a thumb-length thingy and yak away in front of me. That evolution in mores was a few years in the future.

My triumph at selling the Jane Austen set was diminished by my inability to point out the buyer. “What does he look like?” the dealer asked. “I don’t know what he looks like. He’s just your typical retired Microsoft executive,” I answered unhelpfully. A Seattle native, I was nonplussed by a rich techie’s impromptu splurge.

The following year she hired different assistants. For the catalog she laid hold of a *New Yorker* copy editor, while someone with UN experience helped out in the booth. New York abounds in such people, who even at the lower level have accumulated two or three degrees and held prestigious, if not powerful, jobs.

Perhaps this year she will be overseeing someone with both UN and *New Yorker* credentials. I’ll stop by to chat, but most of my time will be spent looking at the books.

Flea Market the Ticket to Clutter

AntiqueWeek, February 15, 2010

We got off to a late start last summer. The six 30-gallon tubs we bought at Home Depot had been lent to someone who was moving. It was the friend of a friend—no one connected with the shop—the details were a little vague. We did not know, for example, where he had moved to. Bushwick, it turned out. Weeks later he showed up with the tubs. Flea market season had begun.

We're eBay vendors. We list and list and—when times are good—ship and ship. Back then, we weren't shipping very much. Revenue was down and we had run out of storage space. The heaps of extraneous objects that cluttered the shelves and filled the basement were depressing. Some were damaged but most were insufficiently valuable to justify listing.

How we ended up with so much out-of-scope inventory requires an explanation. Our supplier does estate cleanouts. The big pieces are sold at an Upper East Side gallery and the smalls come to us. It's a family business. Rather, it's two family businesses working together. Every week a delivery is made, conveying the message: This is what we think of you.

Incalculable hostility is represented by the crayon-on-paper chronicle of a schoolboy's field trip (we were advised to sell it as folk art). Likewise the abstract-expressionist composition that, when examined out of frame, was signed on the verso "Mikey Jones, Grade 4." Less provocative but equally frustrating are the odd pieces of porcelain, 1970s barware, and glittering blobs of Murano glass—fine objects all, but of little use if you need to meet a payroll of five.

The flea market was the answer, but it had to be a real flea market, not one of those weekend assemblies of jugglers, face painters, and organic honey vendors that are popping up in Brooklyn schoolyards. In New York City, there is only one place that qualifies. For years the Hell's Kitchen Flea Market has been a destination for collectors, eccentrics, and obsessive types. It used to be a lot bigger, but the neighborhood was built up and gentrified, so the market is now squeezed into fewer lots. For a time it even looked as if the parking garage might be lost, but it was saved from development due to the financial collapse.

It was in the garage where we set up our booth. No need to provide local color. Like I said, it is a parking garage. One dealer, one parking space is the typical distribution. The fine arts set up along the perimeter where the pipes and wires that line the walls serve as picture rails.

The hours took getting used to. We got there at seven to find the regulars ready to help unpack the week's haul. The first hour was the busiest. The dawn rush over, I sat down to a breakfast of cold tea and congealed egg sandwich. This was the moment for my neighbor to pop his head around the corner and say, "Ah, life at the top!"

I report without vanity we were a terrific success. The reason: an endless supply of fresh stock. Not to mention we were unhampered by all those complicated retentive feelings. Absent as well were the normal profit calculations. Sure, we wanted to make money, but this was stuff we found lying around the warehouse. Who knows how much had been paid for it.

Let's face it: we had the good cheer of people who are protected from risk. Not for us the weekly trawls of the Salvation Army. Nor did we endure a long midnight drive and camping out in the van. At the end of the day we looked forward to a guaranteed per diem and sleeping at home.

Monday through Friday I fill in hundreds of little cells on a color-coded spreadsheet. Customer emails range from pedantic to vindictive ("You are a disgrace to the Meissen community"). At the flea market I got back in touch with the emotional side of collecting. I saw the longing and panic. Somebody's heart beat a little faster at the sight of the stuffed-leather pig with straw coming out of its bottom. The UPS man had been tripping over it for months. We were happy to see it go to a good home. Another case of love at first sight: the Dante bust with a jagged hole in the right temple. It was taken straight out of our arms while unloading the car.

Other objects required compromise; that is, lowering the price until someone took it off our hands. The China Trade covered dish (cover missing) fell into this category. We never took personally the undesirability of our merchandise—on the contrary. Getting rid of the stuff at any price freed up bin space for the following week.

One surprise was the social similarities between the flea market world and the Park Avenue world. The gossip, banter, and jockeying for position that go on in the

Seventh Regiment Armory also go on in the parking garage.

We also had the same types of collectors, including the know-it-all, the therapy seeker, and the silent surveyor. The last are the men who stand in front of a booth and wordlessly and comprehensively appraise the inventory. Their steady, unembarrassed gaze brings to mind the scene in *The Man Who Knew Too Much*, when the assassin shows up at Jimmy Stewart's hotel room.

There were differences, of course. I thought that the flea market experience could have been improved by a dozen waiters in black tie circulating with wine and cheese. But no vendor goes hungry or thirsty. At noon deliverymen whisk by with takeout menus, and one entrepreneur has mounted an old Coleman cooler to a wagon. He loops around every few hours. Just when I thought I was going to faint from the heat, he would reach into the cooler and pull out an iced Coke.

One day I noticed that the proprietor of the drinks cart was also the bathroom attendant. This was not in the job description. Then again, lots of things I've encountered in the past eighteen months are not in the job description. At the top of the list: the worst financial crisis in thirty years.

Just how much things have changed is revealed by the email archive I took over from my predecessor, whose tenure coincided with the mid-decade boom. "Thanks for the bonus. I agree that weekly sales should be at least $20,000" reads one typical message.

Online sales picked up after Labor Day. The dollar was low and there seemed to be more optimism about the economy. We weren't grossing any twenty thousand a week, but the hemorrhaging had stopped. The months of stagnation were over. It no longer made sense to do the flea market every week. Once or twice a month is the new frequency. The basement is overflowing with stuff, so it looks like the flea market will be part of our business model for many more months. I'm looking forward to it.

Salvage Memories

I had no experience working with architectural salvage, but I was in need of money and diversion (principally money). I applied for the job and was hired. Here are my memories of that winter.

I worked as a cataloger in a warehouse that had one floor for plumbing fixtures, a second for doors and shutters, and a third for furniture. The ground floor was reserved for the showpieces, some attributed to this country's finest architects. "Designed by Stanford White for a Westchester Mansion" read one tag. Outside in the back lot were the bathtubs and metalwork. The terracotta fragments suggested an old graveyard. In the snowy twilight you could pretend you were at Père Lachaise.

Inside was dreamlike. The sensation of being in a surrealist film was most powerful in the stairwell, a crowded and shadowy space that was hung with theater backdrops. Not that I ever dreamt about the place. This may have been due to exhaustion. We spent a lot of time outside. The new inventory was unloaded in front of the store and propped against the wall for preliminary documentation. It was hard work. There was a lot of hopping in place to keep warm.

I learned a lot during those months. Until I worked with salvage, I had never really understood modernism. I had taken classes on it and written about it. But I can say that I did not understand its principles and influence until the freezing day when we had to measure and photograph a truckload of Louis XV boiserie.

I can never again enjoy decors with the same innocence. When standing in a room filled with a dozen mantelpieces you realize that there is no permanence in architecture. I am told that archaeologists tend to be gloomy because they spend their day with fragments. There's a similar effect in the salvage trade. It was sad to see piled up on the sidewalk the ornaments and fixtures ripped from a demolished house. Some of these houses were in ruin, but others had the misfortune to be sited on valuable land. It was their fate to be torn down in favor of the condominiums that were going up all over the city.

The warehouse was located in East Harlem. I spend a lot of time in dodgy neighborhoods. Once I know my way around, though, it's no problem finding a decent place for lunch. Past the auto mechanic offering Cash for Your Car Today and around the corner from the Punjab Party Palace and Khyber Travel Agency, there is usually a guy selling really great panini. In East Harlem, there are no panini carts. There are a few hole-in-the-wall restaurants and a grocery store selling aisle after aisle of frozen foods. Thank heaven for the McDonalds a couple blocks away. It's easy to deride the banality of fast food until you've spent time in a neighborhood so blighted that most franchise owners keep away.

There were social challenges, too. Most of my colleagues were artists, a designation that covered a range of talents and expectations. One was a Katrina evacuee, which reinforced my impression that a salvage yard is a place you come to when something has gone horribly wrong. If a job requires historic or stylistic knowledge never ever seek help from an artist. No doubt, those MFA types studied something useful in graduate school, but distinguishing rococo from craftsman was not part of the curriculum.

One man specialized in sculpting chocolate models of the Ministry of Oil in Iraq. The posts were made of Cadbury and the building of Hershey's chocolate. Because the models were perishable he could not sell them.

Instead he sold the color photos he took of the models. “Photography emphasizes the artifice,” he said. He also photographed abandoned fast-food restaurants. This involved a lot of hours in the library, going through old phone books, and driving around in search of boarded-up Pizza Huts. His work was collected by a few regional museums, and he’d had some one-man shows. But he was hopeless—completely hopeless and a little condescending—when it came to cataloging lighting fixtures. Happy was the day when he announced he was moving to Canada.

At the same time, I liked the customers. In my work as a reporter, I meet a lot people who treat their home with professional detachment. “I haven’t been up here in months,” they say while showing me around for a feature. The salvage shoppers were more sympathetic. They took an intense interest in the details of decorating and renovation. We also had our share of salvage skeptics. “Why pay more for something that is used and old?” they asked, usually with regards to the sinks and toilets. It was a fair question and I’m still working on an answer.

You never knew who was going to walk through the door. One Saturday afternoon a charming elderly couple came looking for a bathroom sconce shade. They had lived in the same apartment since the early 1960s.

The post-ops were one group that I had not seen anywhere else in the antiques trade—women with bruised and swollen faces, who were recovering from the latest nip and tuck. We were sufficiently remote that they could browse incognito.

The crack addicts were an occasional problem. They would stumble in and try to steal something. That was why female employees could not be left alone in the shop. Salvage is a man's field.

The winter I worked there coincided with one of those Hollywood strikes that bring movie production to a halt. Prop rentals were down, but thanks to the low dollar, we had decent overseas sales. There was a lot of foreign interest in our radiators and urinals—midcentury urinals, I should specify. There is no escape from the midcentury revival.

Our biggest client at this time was Ralph Lauren. Every time a Ralph Lauren store opened in Moscow or Dubai, we were contacted to help kit it out with chandeliers and sconces. We were the go-to people for creating a simulacrum of the upper-class American house.

We labored under a cloud of bad luck. We got a lot of parking tickets and it was my job to write letters, explaining away our various infractions. I created a template and filled in the blanks based on the details supplied by the owner. "For that one, say there was a funeral procession. For this one, let's use the fire truck," he would say. The tickets were an everyday evil, but this was a place where things were always going from bad to worse. One day our buyer had his car towed. He was at a remote job site, and arranging transportation back to the office was complicated and expensive. The next day he picked up his car and things seemed to be back to normal. But the day after that he called in a panic with the news that his car had broken down. It seems the motor had been stolen at the tow lot and replaced with an old one.

Some days I wondered when I would have expiated whatever crime I had committed that condemned me to toiling on the chain gang of the New York art world. A few months later I had a salaried position with health benefits. Rejoice! Rejoice!

Remembering George Whitman

Book Source Magazine, March/April 2012

George Whitman, the proprietor of Shakespeare and Company, died on December 14. If you were young and bookish, and happened to be in Paris on a Sunday, chances are you were invited by George to the tea party that took place above his shop.

I attended many times when I was a student in the 1980s. George's Sunday salon was a fixture of the expat circuit. Novelists, au pairs, tourists, and artists met for refreshments and talk. Commentators mull over the future of the bookstore. How can it survive in the face of online sales and coarsening taste? George had the answer: free food.

For some it was the nutritional highlight of the week. There was one painter who lived on the Canal Saint-Martin. I visited him a couple times on his boat. We sat in the cabin, gloved and hatted, our breath visible. Thus it was, no doubt, for many Sunday regulars.

A memorable exception was the pretty and playful English girl. She was a world away from the customary indigence. George had a soft spot for girls, and he knew her father, who worked in publishing. He made her dinner, which he served in another room. Nothing was too much trouble.

The original Shakespeare and Company was a legendary place in the 1920s and 1930s. George Whitman's bookstore, which succeeded to the Shakespeare and Company name in 1964, hosted various postwar writers. Its literary importance was much diminished by the 1980s, but its moral support was invaluable.

To be an American in France in those years meant being quizzed on obscure points of Latin American policy. It meant being told that the American role in World War II was overrated. The waiter who served your *croque-monsieur* complained about his cousin's treatment at the hands of Houston customs agents. And while American friendliness was rejected as superficial, any expression of reserve was a bigoted intolerance of foreign cultures. You couldn't win. In this context, the banality of conversation was a blessing. You arrived bowed by the baker's lecture on nuclear deterrence, and were refreshed sipping punch and talking about the Louvre.

I studied at an American institute. The instruction was first rate, but socially, the place was limited. What American student goes oversees to be with other American students? Actually, many did just that, hanging around the lounge, waiting for the mail delivery.

I also took classes at the Sorbonne, an experience that was intense but isolated. French students are slow to form friendships. My classmates lived with their parents, often in remote suburbs. That I knew very few people was to be expected, but I was surprised to realize how little contact they had with each other outside class.

Home life, such as it was, was with a French family in the Marais. They were fixing up a large apartment and raised money for the renovation by renting out the spare bedroom. Not a week went by when they did not mention that it was a *financial* arrangement.

Thank heaven for Shakespeare and Company. It was open late, even on holidays, and not shut down by political unrest. The shop windows shined brightly through bombings and riots. There was a prolonged transportation strike that winter, which was one of the coldest since the war with ice floes in the Seine. It was a bracing walk, but I didn't mind.

I had imposed on myself a French-only rule for reading, but the bookstore was an exempt zone. Don't underestimate the attraction of the books. There weren't many places to read in English. You were conspicuous at WH Smith, across the street from the Tuileries, after an hour. George generously allowed me to take a book upstairs for a quiet evening.

There was also the attraction of the store menagerie: Baskerville the dog and various felines. Walking Baskerville was a favor requested of regulars and strangers alike. "Where are you going?" George, leash in hand, would ask a departing customer.

This brings me to the one occasion when I introduced my American institute friends to Shakespeare and Company. We met there one Saturday. At George's suggestion, we found ourselves jogging behind Baskerville through the maze-like streets of the Latin Quarter. Not exactly how we planned on spending the evening, but my friends were charmed. Baskerville was hungry, so when we got back the manager gave us ten francs for food. We set off once again, only this time my friends were less compliant. "I can't believe we are doing this. They're not even paying us."

The bookstore's customs were evidently not for everyone.

I did not know George Whitman very well. He was an elusive figure, who stayed on the sidelines at parties, if he attended at all. The volunteers, who worked at the store in exchange for a bed, said he was mysteriously detached, even ghostly. But he occupies a big place in my memories of that year.

Diary of Miami Beach Antique Show

***AntiqueWeek*, February 25, 2013**

January 28

Leave New York in cold and dark. Arrive in Miami; spend afternoon dozing and lunching by hotel pool. Suspect this is not why I was brought to Miami, but can't move. I am stupefied by warmth.

Go upstairs for nap ... big bed with crisp, white sheets in a cool room. Get up and head over to convention center. It feels odd to be walking around in loose kakis and short-sleeves.

I'm replacing a colleague with a knee injury. No time to get a picture ID, so I'm using hers. Will security notice I am not South American? No.

Find booth. Not much to do. I was told to keep track of my hours—not sure how to account for today.

January 29

Set up begins. All boxes are unpacked. This is exhausting and heated work. No tables available until late in the day. No air conditioning because of open doors.

Some sales ... dealers pick through tubs and bubble wrap. Go back to hotel at 6 p.m. Long bath followed by dinner al fresco with colleagues.

It's strange to be hanging out in Miami with people I've never seen outside the shop. Even stranger, hearing strains of nearby Kenny Rogers concert sponsored by Trial Lawyers Association. Something to remember next time HMO rates go up.

January 30

Last day of set up ... booth is not much smaller than store, but it's a challenge to find room for everything. More buying and selling with some pieces bought and sold over and over. Having vague college memories of Keynesian multiplier. Also having vague childhood memories of hot potato.

After work, lobster special with colleagues and their relations—also dealers. Almost cut an artery wrestling with beast (lobster). Head back to hotel before coffee.

January 31
Fair opens at noon. There's a big crowd in the lobby ... not out the door, but a long line nonetheless. Doors open; some break into run. There's so much coverage of people who don't care about antiques, it's easy to overlook ones who do.

Replacements reps make rounds, setting up laptops with inventory spreadsheets. It's a busy day. "Not bad" seems to be verdict. Dealers are reticent, hard to interpret.

February 1
Fair chugs along ... more customers today than pass through the store in a month. There are old faces and new.

"Yes, we are still in business."

"No, we have not died."

A Replacements rep waves as he passes, pushing a loaded dolly. Wendy Moonan, former *New York Times* columnist, stops by booth. Spend day doing eBay.

February 2
I'm enjoying this life. Not so much doing out-of-town show, but doing show in *Miami*. I don't have to be at the convention center until 11:30,

so morning routine is leisurely: get up at 6 a.m. and head down to dining room at 7 a.m.

Buffet breakfast: smoked salmon, bacon, sausage, pain au chocolat, fruit, and yogurt. Read and enjoy room, which is large and high-ceilinged with dark wood. Table looks out on pool and palm trees. Waitress brings orange juice and says, "A little chilly this morning." Then it's time for a walk, sometimes to the historic district, but most often along beach. The boardwalk is strewn with fat feral cats.

It's my day off. I'm going to Wolfsonian, a museum of modern design. There is an exhibition of Wiener Werkstätte postcards ... poignant scenes of pre-1914 society. Also visit permanent collection—lots of unknown names and original acquisitions. It's more satisfying than galleries of affordable canonical works.

Tea in museum café: white porcelain cylindrical mug with parallel hollow cylindrical handle holding stainless steel spoon, all on rectangular saucer. *Willow* it's not.

February 3
Spend morning taking sold items off eBay. Some things listed Friday sold here Saturday. To single watcher of our *Gilded Age Sterling Silver Bonbon Server*: you snooze, you lose.

Fair upgraded to “okay.” Infer “okay” way better than “not bad.”

Major discovery: free tea in Ruby Lane VIP Lounge ... *bliss*. Tomorrow is the last day. It’s all hurtling to an end. Soon it's back to the cold and whatever’s moldering in fridge.

February 4

It’s a little quiet, so another long eBay session. I’m not able to upload because supposedly reached monthly listing limit. Not true. Just like eBay to gum up works when trying to achieve B&M-online balance.

The fair ends at 6 p.m. I’m told we’ll be packed up by 8 p.m. Two days to set up, but two hours to dismantle? Not exactly. Furtive packing all day.

At 4 p.m., first distinct sound of a tape roll. Soon there’s a cacophony of tape rolls, box flaps and plastic tubs. Leave convention center after 8 p.m. Pass armored trucks and police cars with flashing lights.

One last walk in tropical night, then it’s back to the hotel.

At Work

Don't Forget to File Your Taxes

***AntiqueWeek*, April 12, 2010**

Many years ago a dealer told me, "I find that when you pay taxes you have less money." True words I reflect upon while tackling a stack of W-2 and 1099-Misc forms.

I'm filing at the last minute because it was necessary to issue a revised W-2. The original had not included my flea market wages. No kidding, I thought. Consider how the money was made: Every weekend, we showed up at the market with boxes of bric-a-brac. The bric-a-brac was converted to money that was used to pay for the space, van, and wages. The profit was deposited in the petty cash box and disbursed for miscellaneous daily expenses. Does the IRS really care about any of this? Guess what—it does. The IRS cares about all money, even the soiled fives and tens that don't get deposited in the bank.

The revision didn't cost me anything because it was my boss who paid the payroll taxes. But even before that was decided, I wasn't too upset. I like working for a company that is in compliance with state and federal tax codes.

I just hope the other flea market vendors don't hear about this. It was bad enough when they found out that my job came with health benefits. Well, la dee da. I didn't think I'd ever live that one down. As for payroll taxes, they're at odds with the can't-be-bothered practices of many in the antiques trade. For every dealer who pays his taxes, maintains good credit, and attends the occasional Rotary meeting, there are a dozen who live in the shadows, running a business with no official existence.

Here's a typical scenario: You see the advertisement for an outdoor antiques show. You show up with a vanload of stuff and spread it out on the rented tables. A few hours later the promoter's assistant comes by to collect the booth rent. You pay cash as do the other dealers. In an idle moment you might multiply that amount by the number of dealers. You might even try to guess what the farmer is charging for his muddy field. That's a lot of money changing hands. Better not ask if it's all getting reported to the IRS. In exchange there will be no questions about your sales-tax reporting. You are up to date with your quarterly filing, right?

There are incentives to stay on track in the form of tax deductions. Taking advantage of them is straightforward if you have prior business experience or grew up in the antiques trade. In many cases, though, the dealer doesn't know how to organize the financial side of the business. Besides, the paperwork doesn't seem very important, when it's a one-man, spare-bedroom operation. It's when the business takes off that there are problems. Start filing now and you're like a UFO on a flight-controller's radar screen. The hundred thousand positive feedbacks on an eBay account opened in 1999 are no longer such a great thing.

Put it off too long, though, and you may end up like the dealer I worked for whose haphazard bookkeeping caught up with him. He'd gone off the grid years ago. He had a warehouse filled with inventory, but it was all very informal. Ditto for the employees; most were here illegally from Mexico. There were menacing letters from the IRS. He could not turn to anyone for advice because he was surrounded by people whose finances were just as rackety. He spent most of the day driving around in the truck. He avoided his office, which was filled with cartons of receipts and time cards.

We were paid by check on Friday. I wondered about those checks when it came time to do my taxes. Is it possible to be paid by a non-existent business? Perhaps that means I don't exist. Such are the metaphysics of tax evasion. The simplest thing would have been to ask, but I hadn't worked there in months. My departure was abrupt and acrimonious. That, in my experience, is the biggest problem with these dealers. Their commitment to the staff doesn't extend past the weekly paycheck, and even that is uncertain. In this case, the Mexicans cashed their checks at the dealer's bank. Sometimes they came back empty handed, and that was the signal that we'd all have to wait until the latest financial hole had been patched up.

It reminds me of the Pirandello novel about the man who fakes his death to escape an unhappy marriage. His new life is just as isolated because, officially, he does not exist. He cannot, for example, work or fall in love. If Pirandello were writing today, he might include getting health insurance. It's pretty hard if you work at a non-existent business. That was the case of one young woman, whose first job was at a dodgy local auction house. Every week she was paid in cash. She didn't mind that, but she did want health insurance. To buy an individual policy she was told that she would need a letter of employment on company letterhead from the auction house. The response to that simple request: What letterhead? What auction house?

There tends to be fast turnover at these places. The ones who stick around are often themselves in hiding. They do not have a bank account, and their tax situation is a subject you really don't want to go into. Instead you find yourself saying things like, "If you had ID, you could go to a good check-cashing place."

Of course, cash flow can be a problem even for seemingly stable businesses. One reason 2009 was a good year is because I did not have to threaten to sue for non-payment or squat in anyone's office. That's the low point: you push your way in and dump down in a chair. It helps to bring a book on these occasions, so you have something to do while waiting for the check to be cut. The one time I did that was for a dealer who was punctilious about making me fill out a W-9. It was proof that just because there's a CPA on retainer, it doesn't mean you're getting paid any time soon. Still, I think you're increasing your chances.

Pay your taxes. The deadline is April 15. Sure, you'll have less money but you'll also have fewer problems.

Help the Press Help You

AntiqueWeek, June 7, 2010

They burst into your booth and pester you with questions. One writes down your comments in a spiral-bound notebook while the other takes pictures. You know it's not the vetting committee. They stopped by on the first day. Not to mention, they were better dressed. Could it be that the press has arrived?

Shows play a big role in the antiques trade. As soon as one is over, there's another to prepare for. Probably, too, the subject comes up a lot in your professional reading. But while there are dozens of consumer and trade publications that cover the antiques trade, there are really only two formats for show journalism.

The first are the preview articles. These tend to be written far in advance. Years ago, I did a bunch for one of the big magazines. The editor would call and—after apologizing for the last-minute rush—assign me to write about a show that was taking place in six months. I sent a request for information to all the exhibiting dealers, who promptly supplied object descriptions and images. I arranged the information and inserted a couple quotes about the state of the market. They were short articles, never exceeding five hundred words. Still, they were time consuming to write. There were four or five drafts to go through before the editor was satisfied. Many changes involved giving prominence to dealers the editor deemed "nice," which was code, I assumed, for "he advertises with us." The finished piece wasn't much to read—mere blocks of text to fill in the white parts surrounding the pictures.

Then there is the reporting, which is usually published in the trade papers. In the old days, when I was writing for the competition, I would go around with the editor before the show opened to the public. Caterers and florists would be scurrying back and forth. There was the hum of the vacuum cleaner. In the distance was the promoter red faced and in shirt sleeves. "How's the show going," we'd ask a dealer stooped over a crate. "It's going great. Sales are good," he'd answer without interrupting his unpacking. We went booth by booth. Most dealers were cooperative, but occasionally, we'd meet with hostility due to a long ago error or a badly placed advertisement. Once we were driven from a booth in a scene reminiscent of an *Expulsion from the Garden of Eden.*

The big shows took four or five hours. By the time we were finishing up the last aisle, the waiters had arrived. "If we stick around, we can get some chow," the editor would say. But we never did stick around for the chow. I had to get home to assemble the story and the editor had dozens of photos to sort through and crop. There would be some follow-up emails to dealers, but the legwork was done. Because most sales were to the trade, the editor reasoned, we weren't missing much by making the rounds early.

He was right to the extent that a show report is an illustrated pricelist. But to be worth reading it needs to be more than a compilation of who sold what. Ideally, it should also convey the character of an event. This is where you come in. Good reporting is collaborative. It depends on the facts and insights provided by the sources. Regardless of when the reporter shows up (my preference is for the last day), it helps to keep in mind certain points.

To start, elliptical and monosyllabic remarks are difficult to interpret. "How's the show going?" may be the reporter's standard opening line, but it usually doesn't elicit much more than this:

Dealer 1: "Sales are better than a while ago."

Dealer 2: "I'm happy."

Dealer 3: "I've seen worse."

With persistence the reporter learns that Dealer 1 switched to midcentury furniture after twenty years in Victoriana. Dealer 2 is a retired tax lawyer who loves her new hobby selling vintage movie posters. Dealer 3 started working the flea markets in the 1970s and does thirty shows a year.

Provide examples of what has and has not sold. Be specific. Describing a painting as "oil on canvas"—as did one dealer—is not helpful.

Opinions are always welcome, especially punchy and funny ones. The important thing is to substantiate your remarks. Yes, the economy is bad, but saying so isn't reporting the news. Explain how your business has been affected by the crisis.

Here's more advice: challenge the myths. For example, young people are not interested in buying antiques. At every show, dealers tell me this. For years, I have been including these statements in my reporting. But how true is it—not to mention how do you know how old anyone is anymore? I'm often off by as much as twenty years. In New York, haggard thirty-somethings are only slightly less common than wrinkle-free seniors.

Sometimes dealers misunderstand the type of information the reporter is looking for. In the middle of telling a perfectly innocuous anecdote, they break off abruptly with the statement, "I don't want to say anymore." It's a familiar experience to reporters and one that reinforces the axiom that everyone has something to hide. Be assured that the reporter is interested only in your professional experiences. That you were late with the March mortgage payment or got a parking ticket that morning is outside the scope of the interview.

More common is the fear of being misquoted. In my experience, this fear is justified. I'm not going to defend sloppy reporting, but I would like to point out that covering a show involves talking to many people. And yes, sometimes there are mix-ups. It's also the case that dealers don't always remember what they said or even that the interview took place. At the big shows dealers may speak to many reporters. Even the most attentive can get confused. Puzzled by a quote attributed to you in the press? Contact the editor or reporter to clear things up.

We sometimes miss a booth. Don't take it personally. If you've been overlooked and want to have your say, track down the reporter. The promoter should have a list of who is covering the show. Most reporters are happy that someone wants to speak to them. Getting the facts straight sometimes requires follow up questions. This can take time, but there is a payoff. In a few weeks, you'll get to read an informative account of the show. Perhaps, you'll even get to read about yourself.

Hiring Decisions

You don't go into the antiques trade to get rich. To survive, though, you need to make a profit. Logically, you expect hiring decisions to reflect this fact. It doesn't always work that way.

One day someone gives notice or you realize that things aren't getting done. You post a help-wanted ad on Craig's List. Five minutes later, the applications start pouring in. Now all you have to do is evaluate the applicants' qualifications against the job description. Actually, sorting through a stack of CVs can be an emotional experience.

The first cull is of the hopeful and inexperienced who "like antiques and could draw on their experience marketing medical textbooks." There is also a "No" pile made up of the embarrassingly overqualified. The job market is so bad that for fifteen bucks an hour you can hire someone who has a PhD and published a couple books. I've never seen a

Rhodes scholar apply for one of these jobs, but it's probably just a matter of time.

Next are the borderline cases, the ones with relevant experience who might have a chance with family connections or a strong economy. They often seem like good company and would probably form the pool for a successful dating agency: Mr. Trench Master of the Pont-du-Gard Aqueduct Dig, meet Miss Archivist of a Private Collection of Futurist Ephemera. But matchmaking isn't your thing. More pertinently, the economy is in the toilet and they're not related to you. So you toss them.

With luck you'll end up with five or six applicants who merit an interview. Deciding whether one applicant's experience working as an exhibition assistant is a better fit than another's editing a price guide is a challenge, but it's easier than gauging social compatibility. Dealers say they want employees with a demonstrated commitment to the trade, but hiring decisions are often based on subjective criteria.

The financial crisis was a grim fact of business when we hired an assistant last year. In those dark days we needed to list more objects on eBay if we were to pull through. We did not hire the person most able to help us do that. All sorts of things got in the way. Take the number one applicant. She had worked in a regional auction house, while attending an obscure college. In the owner's view, her alma mater canceled out her professional experience. So we sent her a rejection letter. We also sent one to the number two applicant. It was a shame about her thesis topic.

Of course, qualified applicants are often rejected for a good reason. "No, we can't have her," a colleague said about one who had worked in a resort gallery and was active in her family's charity. Nothing wrong with that, I pointed out. This is New York. There's no way to avoid people with money and status. At my insistence, we had her in for an interview. She was awful. She wanted the job, she said, because it would leave her plenty of free time to plan her wedding. It just goes to show that stereotypes are sometimes justified.

In the end, we hired a young woman with the right academic and professional affiliations. She was earnest and hardworking but knew nothing. I don't exaggerate. Four years at an Ivy League school followed by two years of specialized graduate study left her unequipped to distinguish Doric from Corinthian. But this isn't really about the person who is hired but the person who does the hiring. In our case, we were hemorrhaging money and the owner's biggest fear was a socioeconomic mismatch. It makes you wonder why you were hired. A source of pride becomes a source of self-doubt. You mean human resources decisions are not based on knowledge and experience? Well, that's very interesting.

The first time I witnessed a hiring decision as an accommodation of private needs was a world away from the shabby Brooklyn warehouse where these scenes took place. It was on the Upper East Side in a historic institution. The search had been narrowed to two applicants when the committee met. The first applicant fulfilled all the requirements. The second was the director's friend, another of the middle-aged homosexuals she conspicuously favored. According to the director, her friend's personal qualities outweighed the twenty-years' experience of the other. For proof she told the following story: at a dinner party, someone made an awkward comment and her friend handled the situation with grace. And so, he was hired. It's worth noting that the qualified applicant had grown up in Soviet-occupied Europe and come to this country alone. But she inspired no special sympathy. Her hardships didn't compare with what the director's friend had gone through. That must have been one humdinger of a dinner party.

The director's friend is an example of a second-tier applicant who more or less worked out. But if he hadn't, it wouldn't have really mattered. A place like that doesn't need to make a profit. Just send the fundraiser out for a round of squeeze-the-millionaire. Dealers don't have that option. The antiques trade is a tough business. It would be less tough if dealers made serious hiring decisions.

Blogging and other Distractions

Remember 2008—pretty awful, wasn't it? We weren't sure we were going to make it. Sales were down two-thirds from the mid-decade peak. That was devastating, but what really shook our confidence was the lurching about from one recession-busting scheme to another. No sooner had we tried free shipping then it was yanked in favor of lowered prices. Only the blog was safe.

Ah, the blog.

Have you ever bought an antique after reading a blog? Me neither. In a rational world, that would be sufficient to kill it. But a persuasive webmaster ensured that the blog lived. Let's give credit, too, to the owner's desperation and her long immersion in an academic (that is, impractical) milieu. It was going to be the polyphonic sort, with regular contributions by the catalogers. The objective was to raise our ranking in the Internet search engines. That would lead to ... more sales? The logic was shaky but not the resolve.

If an object were not listed on eBay, we had no way to sell it. The unlisted backlog ran into the thousands. Productivity was erratic, and there were a lot of simmering morale problems. Addressing them would have demanded more tact and detachment than the owner possessed. Small wonder she preferred to pin her hopes on the blog.

I am not opposed to blogs. Nor am I opposed to innovation or the occasional alleviation of the daily grind. What alarms me is the search for an escape from the responsibilities of running a business.

The dealers who are strong on logistics are the least susceptible to the promise of the new ideas. They try to move antiques efficiently and profitably through the market. It's an arduous undertaking that leaves little time for fantasy. The "big picture" dealers are the ones I'm wary of. They launch into long speeches on civilizational decline based on weak demand for Victorian berry spoons. Their yearnings and aspirations rarely include competent inventory management.

Because I write, I am a natural target for these special projects. "Let's try something new," my boss will say. Each time I fear (often with justification) that I am going to jeopardize my livelihood. It means double the work because, despite its urgency, a special project never supersedes the daily tasks but must be crammed in between the tagging and polishing. And while a special project typically culminates years of egregious mismanagement, I have never met a dealer who had doubts about deserving such charitable exertions. The financial reward for participation is zero. "I'll do something for you when things are better" is the stock nebulous promise.

Once a dealer assigned me to write a catalog. Catalogs had been a vital sales tool for his business thirty years before. He wanted to recapture the magic by issuing a new one. It wasn't at all a bad idea: a selection of the inventory photographed and wittily described. Just maybe it would work. He negotiated with the neighborhood printer and recruited a layout designer.

There were good reasons why I never made progress on it. For one, the dealer could never make up his mind which objects to include. More troublesome was my growing lack of confidence in the project. No doubt, the money could have been better spent. The website was rickety. Every week or so, we'd get a call from the webmaster telling us that we'd run out of space and needed to take down some images.

Special-project fantasies flourish when the dealer is remote from daily operations. This one spent little time in the store, which meant he was never around when the dunners were threatening to turn off the electricity. The more dire his problems, the greater the expectations he placed on the catalog. The catalog would allow him to pay back the creditors who left menacing phone messages. It would revive interest in his field and attract the notice of the right magazines. That he'd lost his mailing list many years before and didn't know where to send the catalog made all these scenarios unlikely.

I've no idea how the catalog turned out. I was gone long before it was finished. In fact I have never succeeded at any special project. The very instability and lack of realism that foster their conception make them impossible to execute. I am prepared for the next dealer who approaches me with a suggestion to try something new. My answer: "Great! How about clearing off the backlog?" In my experience, that would be something new.

Determining the value of research not always easy

AntiqueWeek, July 16, 2012

It was my first month on the job and I wanted to make a good impression. I was assigned to catalog an art nouveau vase. It was easy to decipher the signature, but an Internet search did not turn up very much. So I went to the library where there was a book on the maker. The book informed me that all the Internet information was wrong. There was a bonus, too, in learning that my vase was rare.

But what was my research worth? The vase took months to sell on eBay, and rare or not, the price was equal to what was paid for other vases by that maker. The time I spent at the library could have been spent more profitably listing other more straightforward objects. Lots of eBay vendors let the pictures do the talking: a concise description with four to six images. What more does the buyer need?

It's an important question if you work in the antiques trade. On the one hand, good research can enhance a dealer's reputation. The customer's "What's this?" can be answered with fluency and confidence. On the other hand, research takes time and time is money. For the small business owner, quick cut and paste may seem like the only way to survive.

Certainly, many of my experiences could be used as proof that research is a money loser. My very best eBay listing was for an object that turned out to be a fake. I spent hours researching and writing but didn't really look at the object.

Another time we were selling a painting by a noted twentieth-century artist. The fine arts specialist casually listed it at a modest minimum bid. A sale seemed certain. Worried that we didn't know enough, I made a trip to the library. Sure enough, based on the catalogue raisonné, I learned that we possibly had a lost painting from an important series in the artist's career. These speculations were included in the revised listing, and the minimum bid was increased. The painting didn't sell. We really needed the money and would probably have been better off letting it go at the original low reserve. In my defense, I assumed the research was only the first step in establishing the painting in the artist's œuvre. Still, I felt responsible that we were stuck with it for years.

The economic value of research is a concept that tends to be associated with the high end of the market. I used to work in a library that was frequented by picture dealers and auctioneers. Their research was focused and expedient. No serendipitous browsing on esoteric subjects—they couldn't afford it. Instead there was an intense and thorough investigation of attribution, provenance, and exhibition history, the areas that were most likely to increase or at least clarify value. Nonetheless there was a limit to what they'd do to get this information.

At one point the library decided to charge an annual fee to the commercial readers. Because the library was supplying financially valuable information, the reasoning went, the library should receive compensation. It was a spectacular failure. In New York there are other libraries that can supply much of the same information, though in less elegant surroundings. As for the unique information, the opportunity to find any was deemed by many to be of less value than the fee (fifteen hundred dollars, I believe). Attendance collapsed. The policy was abandoned but not the principle. Fundraising was pursued indirectly through benefit sales and catalog donations.

At the low end of the market, where multiples predominate and prices are predictable, the argument in favor of research can be summed up in the question: Have you ever had a colleague who does not see the point of research? I have. I've even trained a few. Well, I tried anyway. Nothing really took. They were efficient workers to the extent that they didn't dawdle over the Royal Doulton price guide. But then they didn't really know what Royal Doulton was. This superficiality correlated with a hazy stylistic analysis (anything gold was rococo) and an approximate knowledge of colors and shapes. Nor was there a compensating fund of common sense. One young woman persisted in classifying every shallow clear-glass bowl as a cachepot.

The sensible thing would be to hire someone in the middle. *Not* the one who studies the Wedgwood shape books in preparation for cataloging a collection of jasper Christmas ornaments, and *not* the one who shouts across the store, "Here's a box of blue and white thingies. They need polishing," but the informed and directed researcher with an eye on the clock is the one to hire. Such people are rare. Failing that, hire the bookish introvert and allow time for spontaneous and questing researches. But don't allow too much time.

Mentalities

Trade versus Museum

Nine or ten years ago, I read the announcement that a dealer had been hired as a curator at a midwestern museum. I knew the dealer, a specialist in old master paintings. He was notorious for his rages at the library where I used to work. There were red-faced screaming fits over missing *Burlington* issues that ended with him storming out. Sometimes, like a horror-movie monster, he would burst back into the reading room, his fury undimmed. It was hard to imagine him working in a museum. Did he possess the necessary self-repression? I had my doubts.

The art world has many traditions, but one of the most enduring is the separate paths of museum people and trade people. There is rarely any crossover past the early years of internships and part-time jobs. A profile of people who made the switch seemed like an interesting magazine feature. I began cutting out related career announcements. I never accumulated more than a handful. One involved a museum with famously eccentric hiring practices. Another was for a curator turned auction house appraiser. This looked promising until I realized that his expertise was in an esoteric field where overlap is perhaps inevitable. My scant results confirmed what I had observed: there is no routine back and forth. A curator might go work in a library or historical society, but the commercial world is pretty much off limits. Likewise, a dealer going to work in a museum is newsworthy.

I was first exposed to the trade-versus-museum divide while working in the library, where the dawdling pace and wordless penalties proved too much for many dealers. Their researches tended to be expedient and specific, and were undertaken with detachment. Nothing wrong with that. But the staff identified with the in-depth and long-term projects undertaken by the scholarly readers—the dissertations and books that years to write.

Most regulars, though, were dealers who included the library in their daily circuit. The library's funding was partly dependent on these visits, but there was no great bond. The separation was rooted in an antitrade bias. Many institutions are discreetly active in the art market, and the deaccessioning scandal suggests a cadre of curators who wearily view the reserves as so much slow-moving inventory. Nonetheless, you meet with the view that while studying the art market is an ennobling activity, real life buying and selling is not nice.

My colleagues did not come to this view without help. Many had attended a school that was a locus of antitrade sentiment. There was one anecdote the alumni told about a promising student who'd been lavished with mentoring and scholarships. After graduation he threw it all away to work for a dealer *and his name was never mentioned again by the professors*. True or not, the story was widely circulated.

In a similar line, I recall the experience of one young woman who was a student at this school and accepted a job at Christie's. She had been working at the library as a part-time research assistant. While the auction house job was just as lowly, there was the possibility that with luck and grit she would be able to leverage all that learning into a real career—something that would never happen at the library, no matter how many years she stayed. Congratulations seemed to be in order—but not so fast. "I don't think I'll be putting Christie's on my resume," she said before she started. She lasted only a few weeks. She was done in by the aggression and turmoil. Surely, though, another very small reason for her failure was the absence of encouragement from her academic advisers.

At the library, she had worked on a checklist of Spanish artists that the library had drifted into committing to produce. It was a big, messy, and completely unnecessary project that was undertaken in honor of the Columbus quincentennial in 1992. While the work was begun years in advance, the first volume was published only in 1993, with three more still to be completed. Here was the reverse of the hasty research presumed to flourish in the commercial world.

The perception of time is different in institutions. In the ten years it takes an assistant curator to get settled, a dealer will have burned through three or four jobs. At the library the slow turnover contributed to the formality. Relations were characterized by a mix of venom and idealism. There was fastidiousness about social and professional qualifications. Institutional morale was dependent on spending the day with colleagues of the right background. At the same time, people were intensely competitive and, while finding reassurance in their colleagues' achievements, strained to outshine them. The watchfulness brought to mind the Bastille memoirist who wrote, "There are no observers more attentive than prisoners."

I left the library to work in the rare book department of an auction house. It was one of those places where people say what they think. That was hard to get used to. Different, too, was the way the people spoke about themselves. At the library, I had been accustomed to working with fantasists, but the high level of corroboration was a check on self-aggrandizement. I once mentioned that, according to family tradition, I was a collateral descendant of Daniel Boone. A year later, completely out of the blue, a colleague reported that based on his study of the Boone family history, it was probably true.

The habits of verification took root during these years, but they were thrown away at the auction house. No point in sitting down with *Who's Who* to sort through the gush of personal revelations. Unchallenged autobiography was one of the perks of the job.

A print specialist who started around the same time made all sorts of farfetched assertions: She could pen thoughtful and scholarly catalog essays. She was a natural at client relations. She was a zealous copy editor who never lost sight of the big picture. She was both all-rounder and specialist. At the library, these pretensions would have been punctured with a tart "Goodness, aren't you clever." Far from expressing a minimum of doubt, the people in charge promoted her to director.

They made no attempt to substantiate her claims. Most glaring was the flagrant unlikelihood of such gifts being nurtured at the obscure local auction house where she had worked for ten years. Her meager talents were evident after only a few weeks, but the deception was never a cause for resentment. Who knew the difference? Not to mention she had a genius, for once not imaginary, for praising the pretensions of others. Pretensions that were as absurdly inflated as her own were met not with silent skepticism but effusive admiration.

Chalk one up for the museum world. They wouldn't have been taken in. While you occasionally encounter stagey self-deprecation in these places, there is also a touching modesty. Years ago I interviewed a curator who had written a catalog and organized an exhibition on Victorian furniture. Despite these accomplishments, she did not consider herself very knowledgeable about Victorian furniture. She went out of her way to emphasize her lack of expertise.

That scrupulousness extends to office politics as well. All institutions have their toads and liars not to mention the plain unobservant. But it's usually not difficult to establish what happened at the last meeting. At the auction house there was no truth. The most vehement carried the day. This is the totalitarian side of the trade. An annihilating force is turned on the most trivial issues. You, in the Winston Smith role, are lucky if you can find one other person who admits to remembering, say, the agreed upon wording for client correspondence. The support tends to be furtive with lots of meaningful eye contact and mouthing of words. Sometimes you can track down supporting documentation. You don't pass it around—there's no question of changing minds—but it's reassuring to know that your grasp of reality has not weakened.

Since I'm listing the things institutions do right, let me add the sense of order. Spending your formative professional years immersed in an ethos of "a place for everything and everything in its place," leaves you completely unsuited to work in an auction house. After one sale there were dozens of leftover catalogs. (My predecessor had pocketed the department Rolodex, leaving us with a truncated mailing list.) I conscripted an intern, and we hauled them to an upstairs storeroom that was a dumping ground for old catalogs. The intern suggested tossing them and slamming the door. No, I said, we must put them in the right place. We surveyed the tottering stacks and torn cartons. Then it was down on our hands and knees to clear a space against the wall—a patch of order amidst chaos. Better to have followed the intern's advice. That would have shown an effort to fit in.

I have had many jobs. The auction house was the worst, but elsewhere in the trade there's the same corner cutting and volatility. No place is perfect. The library had many problems, though there was a compensating intellectual seriousness. Very superior the library people were, especially the women. No slatterns or blowzy types worked there. I've encountered this superiority in most of my dealings with museum personnel. A call to the PR department about an upcoming exhibition is answered by a voice redolent of neatness and precision. Perfectly ordinary exchanges in a commercial setting (e.g., "I'm getting a tattoo this weekend." "Yeah, me too.") are unthinkable in these places.

Nonetheless the library was a unique chapter in my life—not only because the library was unique (very unique, indeed), but because I have never made more than desultory efforts to get back in the fold. I wanted to write. This was impossible at the library. You'd think a place where words like "panoptic" and "habituate" were bandied about would be ideal. Not at all because it seemed presumptuous in light of my better-educated colleagues' ambitions. They too had big projects in mind. But all their learning was never enough. One more language, maybe even another degree was always necessary. I was surprised to discover that upon finishing a PhD, some had turned right around and started over on a second MA. You can see that as an example of sterling integrity or monumental procrastination. The atmosphere of winsome sadness and muted anger was stifling. The jostling, hectoring, and approximate world of trade proved more stimulating.

When I feel the paralysis of writer's block descending on me, I check out Craig's List for an inventory or fair job. I'm up for anything except the auction house. Not that. Never again.

Are you sure those were the days?

For a reporter, covering a show can be tricky. Dealers are reluctant to exult when things are going well. Put it down to modesty or superstition or the trade's rich tradition of pessimism, but dealers tend to downplay the highs. At the same time, they downplay the lows. "It's a great chance to make contacts" and "The promoter has brought together a good group of dealers" are remarks that can be intended to conceal less than stellar sales.

Recently, when I go around with my notebook, I've been hearing something new: "Things are okay, but it's not like five or six years ago." Five or six years ago would be 2005 and 2006. Was that a golden age? That wasn't my impression. On the contrary, I remember a lot of talk about what "a great chance it was to make contacts."

I cover the New York market. Back then, 9/11 was an unhealed wound. The armories that host the city's most important antiques shows were no longer imposing edifices with fine woodwork and old portraits but places to train war-bound soldiers. While the recession was over, economic confidence was weak. All in all a difficult time. But compared to today maybe it wasn't so bad.

Good memories are important. They're the vital fallback when you're slumped in your booth, watching show goers carry away the armloads of merchandise that they bought from the competition. But good memories can be dangerous when they are associated with normalcy. You work hard. Sales are good. The money is coming in. Is it too much to ask for that to continue? Yes, it is because the good times are the exception in business and life. Not to mention, memories—good or bad—do not always accurately reflect events. Diarists will know what I'm talking about.

I used to work at an eBay business that was founded in the early years of the Internet. For online vendors it was an exceptional time. Prices held steady, costs were reduced, and the one-man, back-bedroom operation now had a global reach. That era ended for reasons that are familiar to readers of the trade papers: changing tastes, aging collectors, and in the glut of objects flooding the Internet, a new insistence on flawless condition. My colleagues didn't read the trades.

I started working there in 2008. The economy had not yet gone off the cliff, but sales were down in quantity and price. Nonetheless, I was instructed that discounts should not exceed 10 percent on objects that were priced at 2000 levels. Structural changes in the market? They hadn't noticed any. Someday things would return to normal, they believed. Normal, in their experience, was the turn-of-the century boom. Happy days of easy sales and giddy morale. "You should have been there," they said.

I was a tad skeptical of my colleagues' nostalgia. I have been working long enough to know that even the best workplace has problems. Plus I had documented proof that this one was no different. The specialist I replaced had been the office manager. I inherited from him a big inventory (he had complete faith in the market's eventual recovery) and an email account dating back many years. Occasionally, I would dip into the archives and read about the difficulties in obtaining inventory and meeting sales goals—difficulties that were still the subject of tense meetings and long phone calls.

These mundane concerns had no place in the reminiscences, which emphasized the bonuses and celebrations. Certainly, they had fun. There were several fulltime employees listing, photographing, and shipping antiques from a shabby row house. They were drawn from the ranks of photographers and novel-writers that colonize Brooklyn's slums. Providing so many with a salary and health insurance was in the domain of social work. But an office staffed with free spirits presents special HR challenges. One undercurrent of these tales of yesteryear was the volatility. "We changed the passwords after she left" was the windup to one anecdote. Another was that they described events that took place ten years before. Subtract ten years and you'll find many memories take on a rosy tinge.

Don't get me wrong. I would much rather have worked there in the early years. Salaries were higher and eBay had fewer fussbudget rules. More than anything, I would have enjoyed the freshness and momentum. No wonder my colleagues remembered that time as special. Everyone should have a golden age to look back on. It's usually a mistake though to assume that it can be revived or that it was completely golden.

Men are better hoarders, women more likely to disperse

AntiqueWeek, April 1, 2013

Hoards come in all sizes. An example of the small hoard is the communal coin cache you never fail to find working for an estates dealer. At my old job, it was kept in a blue shoebox on the bookcase in the back room. Into the box was emptied all the spare change found in the various receptacles that passed through our hands. It was a decade-long accumulation, but by the time I got there, most of the quarters were gone. I made my way through the dimes and nickels and left the pennies to my successor.

Then there are the big hoards. In today's market, the object of desire is as likely to be the land beneath the store as the inventory inside. You see them in big cities: a lone antiques store surrounded by condominiums, supermarkets, and Pilates studios. The proprietor bought the building decades ago, when the neighborhood was rundown. Property values rose steeply. His wife and children have been after him for years to sell out, but the old boy holds on. He enjoys the power that comes with sitting on 20 million dollars of urban real estate. Not to mention, he has a place to go during the day to escape the hovering and restrictions that accompany old age.

I visited one such dealer once a week for two years. He presided over a gallery where the daily bustle never completely obscured the long-term calculations. I worked for his daughter, who was an eBay vendor. The purpose of the visits was to obtain inventory for her business. I was trained in this and other responsibilities by the man I was replacing. He had held the job for four years. On the first visit to the gallery, he introduced me to the dealer and his staff. We spent an hour standing around and talking. The gallery was the neighborhood salon and people dropped by to chat. We then spent another hour picking out pieces. The staff had put some out for inspection but most were of insufficient value. They let us take what we wanted. In the subway, on the way back to the warehouse, I was given all sorts of advice about negotiating with our boss' father.

The necessary mix of tact, deference, and companionability were foremost in my mind the first time I went there on my own. The week's objects were left by the door. They weren't very good, but I was not comfortable rummaging through the inventory on my own. There was no one to speak to apart from the dealer, who was dozing behind the desk. I signed off on that batch and returned to the warehouse. I hoped that the following week would be more fruitful. It wasn't. They started putting the objects outside, so there was no need for me to go inside the gallery. Gone was the collegiality that prevailed with my predecessor. "Do you have a question?" they'd ask politely. After six months, someone ventured to inform me that "there are books with prices and information about antiques." And eight months after that, I was told that "if you turn a dish over, there is a mark that tells you who made it."

Clearly, they did not accept me. But this was about more than hurt feelings. If we didn't get good inventory, we couldn't meet our costs. Thus began the ruses and maneuvering. One suggestion bandied about at the warehouse was that I would simply take what I wanted. But wouldn't that be stealing? I imagined myself running from the police with a Capodimonte lamp hidden under my coat. Once, in a never to be repeated experiment, the dealer's daughter (my boss) came to the gallery. It set back the cause by seven weeks. A truce was reached when the dealer's wife exerted pressure. She was in charge of payroll for her husband's business, a fact that ensured we obtained enough Herend cachepots and Victorian letter racks to keep going.

Socially though, the visits continued to be strained. I reluctantly point out that the gallery was staffed exclusively with men while on our side it was all women. The humiliating junior-high standoff confirmed what I had long ago observed: men are better hoarders than women, who are often feared as hoard dispersers. Give a woman a foot in the door and she'll sashay around, tidying and sorting, like Jane Powell in *Seven Brides for Seven Brothers*. Before you know it, the porcelain will be in one place and the silver in another, and all the mystery will be gone.

Back at the warehouse, the fine arts specialist liked to speculate on the gallery's reserves. The gallery basement, which was off limits, was filled with paintings. That these paintings were superior to the horrors they gave us every Wednesday was an article of faith. Unquestioned, too, was all the money we would make if we were ever allowed to sell them. "We imagine it to be a Shangri-La, but what if that's not true?" she said in a rare moment of doubt. Indeed, it was possible the masterpieces in the basement would turn out to be clown studies and Trevi Fountain watercolors, just like the ones we were already listing on eBay.

In the absence of proof, we reverted to our optimistic assumptions. Like most hoard fantasies, they required deferral. In this case, it was the fine arts specialist's reluctance to move on in her career until she learned what was hidden away. Good luck with that, I thought. Even if we gained entry, it would take years to find the buried treasure.

On second thought, make that decades. The gallery staff liked to clear paths by shifting around the tottering piles. One day they exposed a door in a wall that lead to a room that was, they told me, half as big as the gallery. This secret chamber, too, was filled with objects. Some people might be excited at the prospect of opening the door and discovering what was inside. Personally, I would rather have a shoebox filled with quarters.

Crazy Colleagues

I had recently started a job in the rare book department of a small auction house. The senior specialist was an elderly man with a spotty memory and ferocious temper. He'd been around so long that I'm not sure they realized how strange he was. One day he pointed to his right temple and said, "I look into people's eyes. I know what they're thinking."

I was not afraid. You see, I spend a lot of time in the company of telepathists. In fact, at my previous job, there was a man who would point to his mouth and say, "I can read women's smiles. I look at their mouths and know what they're thinking." He was cerebral and solitary, though of course with that gift you're never really alone. He liked to scrutinize faces. It never occurred to him that someone's expression might change at the sight of a staring skull's head.

I got to thinking about those men after an encounter at work. There was nothing special about it. It was just one more run-in with a guy in a too tight suit and black shoe-polish comb over shuffling towards me in a sputtering rage. The incident made a big impression on my colleagues, though. To reassure them I said, "I've worked with lots of men like that. I'm not even sure he's in my top twenty of nut cases." "Really?" they said. Sensitive to their reaction, I said, "Well, okay, he is in my top twenty."

I take it back. He's not in my top twenty.

Among the many glaring problems that ail the antiques trade—the economic crisis, gas prices, changing tastes—there is the delicate personnel problem. Does going to work feel like you're playing in summer-stock Sartre? As the master of existentialism said, "Hell is other people." Now think what it's like for the customer who, while spared the full blown theater-of-the-absurd group dynamics, none-theless senses something is not right when he steps into your shop.

Perhaps you have noticed that all my anecdotes are about men. In my experience, women are just as irrational as men. For example, I think women make very good depressives. I once worked for a woman who would announce, "I never really felt loved as a child." Some days she was so overwhelmed that she showed up to work hours late. By then the day was advanced, and she struggled to recruit someone to do what she happened to think needed to be done. She was hurt and mystified that she was not viewed as an authority figure.

Nonetheless, in the antiques trade crazy colleagues are typically men, and while they exhibit many individual traits, they also exhibit many general ones. They tend to be analytical but not observant, and ruminate, sometimes for years, on random and insignificant comments. Then there is the mindreading, which in turn contributes to the obsession with truth telling. If what you say does not match what they *know* you are thinking, they will accuse you of lying.

At the same time, they're rightly convinced that large amounts of information are not reaching them. Less than approachable, they're an unlikely choice for confidences. Whatever information does come there way is too late or insufficient or that old standby, a lie. Any news I passed on to the rare book specialist was met with hostility because—I'm not making this up—that was something I had never told him. His fury was due, in part, to the assumption that women are conduits for information rather than partners in conversation.

Come to think of it, for these men, any situation involving a woman is a situation that needs to be brought under control. Those were the words of the rare book specialist (to draw again on that rich experience). He used to scream, "I can never bring you under my control," while spasmodically pumping his fists up and down. Sometimes there were tears in his eyes. His repressive treatment of me was in contrast with his nostalgia for my predecessor, a young man with whom he enjoyed a playful and irreverent camaraderie.

For all his irrationality, including his tirades about the importance of being rational, the rare book specialist was a credible figure at the auction house. Every effort was made to meet the needs of a man who was a bottomless pit of needs. Why? I never completely overcame the suspicion of blackmail. In any case, the ability to inspire loyalty is characteristic of the type.

An extreme case, you say. True, but crazy colleagues are ubiquitous in this business. It would make sense if they had unique expertise, but I have never known that to be the case. Whatever it is they contribute is so precious that it offsets the consequences of a demoralized staff. Think of all the appraisers who do not throw big-boy tantrums. Promote them for a change. That's my take on the problem. Possibly some of you already knew what I was thinking.

The Family Business

If you work in the antiques trade, chances are you work in a family business. Perhaps it's your family that owns the business. You are there through ties of blood or marriage. Or perhaps, like me, you are there through the classifieds. I am a professional foster child who has pretty much abandoned all hope of finding a forever family. Every few years I make a fresh start.

However cordial the relationship with my current work family, my viewpoint is that of an outsider. For the outsider everyday is rich in observations and speculations. You learn, for example, that Grandpa is not the senile paralytic his middle-aged children make him out to be. On the contrary, he pushes himself out of his chair and greets you with a friendly bear hug.

You learn, too, that there is a fine line between investing in a child's career and an intergenerational wealth transfer. There are many reasons auctioneers are holding modern sales, but an overlooked one is the opportunity it represents of bringing in the children. Call about an upcoming modern sale and you'll likely be told, "You have to speak to my son about that."

You struggle in silence with the nature-versus-nurture question. Your secret adoption theory is as impossible to prove as the suspicion that your previous employers were subjects in a cloning experiment.

You contrast your employee discount with the family's right to treat the store as a gift closet. Especially acquisitive was the absentee couple that lived out West, university professors committed to modishly academic politics. The woman liked paintings. The man complained about the crystal. "There's a bubble in the foot."

Sure, outsiders endure slights and neglect, but they possess this one advantage: when things get really bad, they can move on. For family, there's no browsing of the want ads. They're stuck. Ordinary workday tensions and humiliations are magnified. A *Godfather* analogy seems unavoidable: the Tom Hagen role gets old, but be grateful you're not Fredo Corleone. On a related note, the co-owner of a large antiques gallery recounted that when she passed her brother-in-law's parked car, he slumped down in the seat like a mobster ducking gunfire.

The parent-child relationship is especially burdened. There are minor matters, like the weirdness of being on a first-name basis with Mom and Dad. Then there are the major ones. The children often missed out on the heroic years—the slow and difficult rise from the parking lot to the armory. They may be informed and competent but tend to be deficient in the combative charisma exuded by their parents.

Hands down the most oppressive parent-child relationship I've encountered was at an Asian gallery. The owner was a venerable sage, who never left his great desk by the entrance. The porcelain specialist was also in the sage line, and was imbued, I was told, with mystical expertise. One day, the wise men noticed that customer traffic wasn't what it had been. Where had it gone? Sales were down and there was talk of closing the gallery. The owner's youngest son was recruited to see if the place could be saved. His conventional proposals of a website and magazine advertising were not exactly opposed by the elders. Then again, it was hardly a case of all hands to the pump. Things went on exactly as before with the father's contemplative immobility and the porcelain specialist's frequent retreats (that is, cigarette breaks). The poor young man—actually he was not very young at all. He was a husband and father in his forties—spent his days running errands for the old men. He was so put upon that he offered to include me—the Craig's List cataloger—in the daily Starbucks run. I think of those days every time I pass the building. The gallery is long gone. However catastrophic the collapse, it was no doubt experienced with introspective detachment.

At this point, I should define what I mean by family. Two brothers with a shared passion for odd-closure fruit jars do not qualify as a family. A family (in the social sense) must include at least one woman. A dealer told me that in his field most collectors were men, but most sales were to women, and choice was determined by where the piece would go. The room's principal occupant and surrounding objects mattered as much as the buyer's taste. Indeed, women are context creatures.

Gentlemen, if want to succeed in the antiques trade, get married. Your wife will be your link to the outside world. While you shuffle through old clippings to show that the colonial secretary is similar to one in a 1972 *Magazine Antiques* advertisement, your wife will be greeting customers by name and asking how their daughter liked the tea tray. It is the wife who humanizes the work place. She remembers that there is a holiday in December, when it would be appropriate to close the shop and maybe even give the employees a small gift. Bachelor dealers don't do Christmas.

But there can be too much of a good thing. A feminine management style prevailed at my first two jobs, and festering sentimental places they were.

The first was indirectly tied to the trade. It was a library that was frequented by art dealers. It was founded by a Victorian spinster. She gave her life to the library and many employees were happy to reciprocate. The atmosphere was domestic and insular. After her death, continuity was ensured by the descendants of her fertile relations, who acted as trustees. A society magazine once published the family tree. It was not Xeroxed—trademarked phrases were discouraged—it was *photocopied* and distributed to the staff.

Daily operations got a bit off track over the years. A new director was hired to revitalize the institution. In this she was successful, though she perpetuated the cozy, cuddly HR practices. She liked to make surprise hires of all the special people who'd wandered into her life. One important job was filled by a man who had written get-well emails to a sick friend. "They were so thoughtful and witty." I never heard her offer any other reason for the choice. She had tradition on her side, though the heaving and trancelike praise of her favorites was tiresome.

I thought, "I work in a personal place where they make personal decisions. I want to work in a business where they make business decisions." I got half my wish. My next job was in a business where they made personal decisions. It was, you might not be surprised to learn, a family auction house that was under the direction of the nice widow lady who'd taken over after her husband's death a few years before. Mother loved all her children, but she was most accommodating of those who required accommodation. The narcissistic rages of the man I worked for elicited her nurturing sympathy. For his victims there were cajoling hugs. Loving Mother! She never judged. Unconditional acceptance was Mother's way.

I had gone from one dystopian matriarchy to another. It was awful, a horrible place that inspired a perverse optimism. At the start of a new job, I think, "Well, it's not going to be *that*." I did not last long at the auction house. The grounds for dismissal were unambiguously personal. I was sent forth into the job market to begin anew. Such are the perils and blessings for the outsider in a family business.

The Top Tier: Some Never Get Over Not Getting In

Hartford Courant, July 15, 2009

Of the many misimpressions I have formed living in New York, the most resilient relates to the number of Ivy League graduates. My estimate—erroneous, I know—places the number of Americans with an Ivy League degree at 20 to 25 percent. If you add in the other top-tier colleges, like Williams and Amherst, that figure rises to 40 to 45 percent.

These numbers are pure fantasy, but it's often the case that, weeks and weeks go by before I meet anyone who did not graduate from one of these schools. The question "Where did you go to school" is more likely to elicit for an answer "Brown" than "North Dakota State."

My own academic record is more singular than distinguished. I graduated from Evergreen State College, a school that few people have heard of. In New York, I always explain that it is located in Olympia. And when I am feeling especially communicative, I add that Olympia is the capitol of Washington State. In the hundreds of times I have had this conversation, only two people have ever heard of the place (one was a college counselor).

"Distinctive" was the word chosen by the school's PR department to describe a school that perpetuated the most cherished conventions of the 1960s. Points of interest included the organic farm and a parking lot filled with the vans and school buses that were inhabited by the least hygienic of an unhygienic population. The co-op, where we stocked up on the seeds and grains that comprised our diet, was located off-campus. Shopping there was as inevitable as pairing army fatigues with one of those baggy Guatemalan tunics. Did I mention there were no grades? We eschewed such pernicious rankings in favor of seminars—endless free-for-all occasions for everyone to say the same thing.

I'll stop there. You can imagine the rest or you can read about it. Evergreen is listed in most college guides, though it is significantly omitted from *Barron's Guide to the Most Competitive Colleges.*

Regionally, if not academically, my college years were typical for my family, who tend to stay close to home. I was raised in Seattle, which is just up the road from Olympia.

When I moved to New York in the 1990s, college was a subject that never went away. It was challenging to have graduated from a school no one had heard of. Did it matter? Of course, it did. Only a fool would say otherwise. But for all my self-consciousness I got off easy.

Nothing compares with the pain of those who aspired to the top five or six schools and—"failed" was not exactly the word I had in mind. "Because I can't join the Harvard Club" was the outburst of one young man, who was embarrassed by his affiliation with the University of Chicago.

I once assumed that the disappointment was diminished by broader experience. Since then, I have met people who retain all their life the insecurities of their late twenties. I worked briefly for one such man. "When I was at Yale" was the prelude to a nostalgic reminiscence about his inconclusive coursework at that school a half century earlier. Not a week passed without an allusion to his happy New Haven days. I never heard him mention the state university where he earned two degrees.

One problem is that if you accept the correctness of the academic hierarchy, it means buying into the whole program. If you agree that going to Harvard qualifies as one of life's great events, you must also agree that Harvard preceded by prep school is even better.

It's rare that anyone has checked off all the boxes, but I know someone who came close. An acquaintance thoughtfully and rigorously planned her son's education. When he got to the Andover part of his academic trajectory, I put him out of my mind. I assumed there wouldn't be anything really newsworthy about someone who was so completely on track. One day, when he'd been at Andover for more than a year, his mother mentioned that he was at last settled at school. Before, she explained, he didn't like his house, but he was able to transfer to a better one.

New vistas of anxiety were opened by this remark. Andover isn't good enough. You have to be in the right house, too. Presumably, the residents of this exclusive dormitory grow into contented and secure adults. Something tells me it doesn't work that way and there is some further refinement in the hierarchy—though what that may be I don't know. They didn't teach that at Evergreen. In fact, the alumni of Evergreen and similar schools are usually spared having to think about such things—and that is perhaps a safe place to be.

Hitchcock Antiquing Fantasies

AntiqueWeek, January 20, 2011

Let's be honest: the daily routine of the antiques trade is not very exciting. You drive around in a truck. You pack and unpack. You look things up in books. There's the housekeeping, too. If you work in a shop, you have to maintain the displays. Online vendors have it easier. Their inventory can be stored on densely packed shelves, but it all has to be cleaned and polished for the photographer. Sure, working with antiques is the opportunity to hold history in your hands, but it's also a job where you go through a lot of Windex.

For diversion I imagine how these tasks could be interpreted cinematically. My favorite director for these fantasies is Alfred Hitchcock. I can think of two Hitchcock movies that involve antiques. In *Suspicion* (1941), Joan Fontaine is married to Cary Grant, who pays his debts by selling the Jacobean armchairs that were a wedding gift from her parents. When you know that, you know all. That he turns out to be a murderous cad comes as no surprise. Then there is the scene in *North by Northwest* (1959) when an advertising executive (Cary Grant again) confronts a spy ring at an auction. More resonant, in my opinion, are the Hitchcock movies that can be viewed as metaphors for the antiques trade. Here's my list (Bernard Herrmann soundtrack optional):

The 39 Steps, 1935

Plot Summary: In London Richard Hannay (Robert Donat) gives shelter to a secret agent, who is killed in the night. Accused of her murder, he flees to Scotland. The police pursue him across the moors, but he escapes and arrives at the safe house, a genteel village residence. Inside he is hidden and protected. Outside he sees the police searching for him. He confides in his host, who lets him know that this is no safe house but enemy headquarters.

Trade Tie-in: I have never been accused of murder, but I have been accused of crimes just as heinous. Substitute threatened negative feedback for flight across the moors. My safe house was eBay and it was just as deceptive as the one in *The 39 Steps.* I arrived frightened and exhausted. Here was hope, I thought, before I saw with horror that eBay was on the other side.

Rebecca, 1940

Plot Summary: Joan Fontaine, in another meek beauty role, is a paid companion who falls in love with tormented widower Max de Winter (Laurence Olivier). They marry and return to Manderley, his magnificent house in Cornwall. Poor Joan Fontaine is completely overwhelmed. She creeps around Manderley in her sensible shoes and schoolgirl blouses, haunted by the oppressive memory of the first Mrs. de Winter. Her fear of the beautiful dead wife is stoked by the sinister housekeeper Mrs. Danvers.

Bonus Line: "Everything is kept just as Mrs. de Winter liked it."

Trade Tie-in: Should be required viewing for human resources personnel. Years ago, I was hired to replace someone who was irreplaceable. Nothing had been changed since his departure six months before. On my desk—*his* desk—was a notepad printed with *his* name. Not a day passed without a pining allusion to *him.* The senior specialist, in the Mrs. Danvers role, pointed to the chair I occupied and said,

"There. He sat there when we cataloged the Horace Greeley manuscript."

Foreign Correspondent, 1940

Plot Summary: It's a staple of spy movies: The hero learns vital information at risk of his life. With his back flattened against the wall and eyes widened in fear, he overhears the bad guys discussing something very, very important. Take *Foreign Correspondent* where an American reporter (Joel McCrea) steals into a Dutch windmill. Sometimes hiding in plain sight, other times trapped behind the grinding cogs, he learns—well, never mind what he learns. That's doesn't matter. What matters is that he spends the rest of the movie dodging assassins.

Trade Tie-in: If you've never deployed dramatic espionage techniques at work, you're missing out on half the fun of office life. At my last job, a colleague would gather intelligence by crouching on the steps that lead to the manager's office. Privately, I thought he overrated the risks. Like most people under thirty, the manager was fairly deaf. He could have stood six inches behind her chair, and she would have had no idea he was there. Still, he got a lot of useful information. For example, one day he learned that that the two of us we're going to be fired. It's nice to know about such things in advance.

Lifeboat, 1944

Plot Summary: It's World War II and the survivors of a torpedoed Allied ship struggle to survive in a lifeboat. At first cooperative and resolute, they soon descend to panic, mistrust, and delusion. Weakened by hunger and dehydration, some jump while others are pushed. The rest make fitful efforts to keep going. They have no idea if they are rowing in the right direction.

Trade Tie-in: Whoa! If you don't think this sounds like what's happened in the last ten years, you need to read *AntiqueWeek* more closely. *Lifeboat* is especially apt as a metaphor because there are only a handful of survivors. All the other crew and passengers are at the bottom of the sea.

Spellbound, 1945

Plot Summary: There is a new director at Green Manors, a private mental asylum. But something is not right. He is surprisingly fresh-faced (the role is played by a young Gregory Peck) and inexplicably ignorant of psychoanalytic theory. Ingrid Bergman is the cerebral and self-contained junior doctor who unravels the mystery of his amnesia and cures him of his guilt complex.

Costume: A white lab coat

Bonus Line: "I think we'd better put him under drugs for a few days. He looks agitated."

Trade Tie-in: Lots of easy humor here. All shops have their regulars. Sometimes you don't even know their names, but probably you know quite a bit about them. This is the clinical side of customer relations. They deposit information with you that they do not confide in their friends. No doubt, there are days when you feel you are presiding over your very own Green Manors (isn't that the perfect name for a rural shop?). Keep in mind, though, that in *Spellbound* the real crazies are on staff.

Rear Window, 1954

Plot Summary: Jimmy Stewart plays a photographer who is confined to a wheelchair with a broken leg. Bored and frustrated, he looks out the window. The neighbors' comings and goings start to form a coherent narrative. His voyeurism leads him to suspect a man has murdered his wife. He watches the murderer, but sees only part of what is happening. He is distracted by the other neighborhood dramas and his relationship with girlfriend Grace Kelly.

Props: None. Leave the binoculars at home.

Trade Tie-in: You're working a show. You don't have a broken leg, but until your wife gets back from lunch, you're trapped, like Jimmy Stewart. You stand in your booth and watch. You watch the customers. You watch the promoter. You watch the other dealers. Eventually, your attention narrows to two or three scenes.

Here's an old anecdote: I was a dealer's assistant at a Park Avenue show. It was a warm spring. The suit jackets were discarded and there was a lot of fanning with the show program. The exception was a French dealer, who wore a cashmere sweater. He never took it off. This was a source of discreet fascination. "He still hasn't taken it off," whispered the dealer I worked for, when I showed up on the last day. But the lesson of *Rear Window* is that you don't see everything. Who knows what we missed while absorbed by the man in the cashmere sweater. Maybe acrobats tumbled past our booth, or across the aisle, Columbian drug lords were selling cocaine in hollowed out books.

Psycho, 1960

I have a mild and gentle temperament. The only times I felt like hacking away with a knife in the grip of a screeching auditory hallucination were when I was on the phone to the eBay rep. Sorry, Jim.

The Hitchcock prism can enliven every dealer's day.

The Crash

The Upside of a Down Market

AntiqueWeek, June 22, 2009

How much is this worth?" A hand—my boss' hand—reached across my desk to the lamp. It's a good lamp, a reliable source of illumination and, now that it was pointed out, a pretty Chinese porcelain vase. I have to say I had never noticed the lamp, which had been picked out by my predecessor. Our inventory tends to be more Qing than Ming, so I'm guessing that it's worth at most a few hundred bucks. But at this point, who can't use a few hundred bucks?

I'm not sure when the recession began. Things seemed to be limping along last summer, when I got the job—not great but by no means catastrophic. There was the feeling, though, that the good times were over. Sales were down both in number and value, I was told. "Before the financial downturn" was the prelude to some nostalgic reminiscence about the golden era of fast turnover and steady cash flow.

No doubt there had been some softening in the market. We're eBay vendors of estate antiques, selling just the sort of traditional wares that have fallen out of fashion.

Some skepticism was in order, though. Most of my coworkers are in their twenties and it can be hard to gauge what "financial downturn" means to someone born in 1983. Add to that there used to be twice as many employees, listing twice as many objects—objects of better quality—and it's no surprise that business seemed to be shrinking.

A few months later business was shrinking. Really, really shrinking.

Every Wednesday I visit our principal consignor who picks out in advance the week's listings. These meetings can be difficult because he is reluctant to part with anything valuable. His store is packed floor to ceiling with antiques, but he does not really want to sell them. Certainly, he does not want to sell them on eBay, which the last time he checked, ca. 1998, was a venue for low-end collectibles.

That changed, thanks to the crisis. The hostility was replaced by panic. The quality of his picks improved. Small treasures began showing up in the Wednesday haul. I'll always remember the week that Lehman Brothers collapsed. The newspapers were filled with images of stunned and distraught employees stumbling out of the building with their briefcases. We were on the brink. That Wednesday, the dealer brought out a set of Tiffany demitasse spoons. "Would this help? What do you think?" he asked solicitously. I snapped open the case and saw twelve vermeil spoons with ruby enameling. I realized then that there was an upside to the crisis.

Don't get me wrong. The hard slog of 2008 is not something I want to revisit. It was during these months that my boss was eyeing up the office furnishings. In the end, she kept the furnishings and cut my hours. And then there were the meetings. Does any government bureau calculate the economic impact of talking about the recession? In those dark days, we probably spent 20 percent of our time coming up with strategies for dealing with the crisis. Boredom and discouragement were the result.

But enough of the bad memories. I prefer to look on the bright side. Let's start with the big one: here we are. Some days we sell things. Some days we don't. We're squeaking by, though.

There are benefits as well as consolations. For one, while sales are down, so too are eBay fees. We got a call from Artnet, recently, asking if we wanted to advertise on their website. A few years ago we'd tried to get involved with Artnet, but nobody got around to returning our calls. That was then. This time the reps were unfailingly prompt and within days had posted a selection of our inventory. It was a moment of pride to see ourselves on the same page as all the big city galleries.

Once a year we call in an outside appraiser. We can handle most things, but for the unknowns we rely on a semiretired Sotheby's warhorse. Last year she let us know that she probably wouldn't be coming back. The trek out to our Brooklyn warehouse was getting to be too much. Guess what—Brooklyn isn't so far, after all. She came out in March, and a very lucrative visit it was, judging by the prices we got based on her expertise.

In fact, it's a wonderful time to hire as we discovered when we advertised for a part-time assistant. Within hours of posting the ad, the resumes began flooding in. Our deliberations went like this: "What do you think of the one who studied at the Courtauld?" "She was okay, but I prefer the assistant manager of the rare book firm." The applicants were desperate. That's why they wanted to work for us. Still, we were thrilled by their interest. In the end we chose someone with a MA in decorative arts history who had done provenance research for one of the local museums. That may sound like overkill for a fifteen-bucks-an-hour job cleaning and photographing objects, but sometimes a buyer's market works in your favor.

We're eager for the recession to end, but while it lasts, we'll keep coming up with ways to profit from it.

After the Crash

I take the subway to work. A one-way fare is two dollars and twenty-five cents. After lunch, which I bring from home, I buy a chocolate bar. That sets me back seventy-five cents. My daily expenses rarely exceed five dollars and twenty-five cents. Weekends, I go to the grocery store sixteen blocks away. The low prices are worth the trip; besides, the walk saves me the expense of joining a gym. Also to that end, I skip the elevator once a day and climb the stairs to my tenth-floor apartment.

You've probably got your own system. Frugality is a necessity for most antiques dealers. It's also morally compatible with the profession of husbanding old things, so they can be enjoyed by future generations.

How have your financial habits changed in the past year? Mine are what they've always been. I've been seeing a lot of newspaper features, advising us to save money by buying seasonal produce and borrowing books from the library. It looks like people really needed to be reminded of this. No need to feel smug, though. After all, our livelihood depends on the willingness to spend on extras.

There's ambivalence about money in the antiques trade. While we appreciate the thoughtful and selective collector, many sales are to the other type—the buyer with the approximate knowledge and unformed taste, who can inspire secret envy and contempt. He may be rich, we think, but he does not understand what he acquires. It is these people with their easy money and deference to the decorator who were keeping things afloat in New York City.

I do not see many changes in the antiques trade. Sure, dealers feel down, but even in good times they're not exactly a buoyant bunch. Elsewhere the demoralization is severe and enduring.

I live on the Upper West Side. In my building the two-bedroom apartments sell in the million-dollar range with a minimum of 25 percent down. It typically requires two incomes to buy one and keep up with the other necessities—the private school tuition, nanny, and vacations. If you are in your thirties and can afford all that, it means nothing really bad has ever happened to you.

In 2008, something bad did happen. In the early months of the crisis, when I walked through my building lobby on the way to work, there would be four or five neighbors, all men, with no place to go. Sometimes they were minding the children or getting ready to walk the dog. They looked disoriented. Some were unfamiliar and I wondered if they were new to the building. No, but they used to work sixteen-hour days. That's why I had never seen them in all the years they had been living here.

Another memory from that time: the newspapers. While the *New York Times* is delivered to the subscribers' doormat, the *Wall Street Journal* is delivered to the lobby, where they are neatly laid out on the counter by the doorman. In the old days, they would disappear early, tucked under the arms of the law and finance people on their way to the office. After the layoffs, there were usually half a dozen copies that went unclaimed.

This was no ordinary bump in the road. One year on, the talk is less about the economy and more about personal disillusionment. I never heard my friends say, "I am going to be very successful," but it turns out that some were privately nourishing that expectation. The realization that it's not going to happen is a blow. Gone, too, is the big income with, in some cases, little to show for the years of abundance. Many, for example, are still renting.

Buying a place wasn't very important when the money was flowing in.

The men are really hard hit. "I should never have stayed on at Harvard for business school," one told me in the 1990s, in one of those boozy the-worst-thing-that-ever-happened-to-me confessions. It didn't seem like he was held back by the Harvard MBA. Every few years he went from one high-flying job to another. He's another one I now see around the neighborhood during the day. He has a new DIY hobby and likes to talk about paint scrapers. Perhaps he's happier.

With so many out of work, my social life has picked up. When we were starting out, most friends were making two or three times my salary. That's not an insurmountable division, especially at that age. But you do lose touch when they're making ten to fifteen times your salary. There's no fighting it.

I get the occasional visitor to the flea market where I work on Saturday. Long lost friends stop by and are amazed by the place. I don't know how long that will last. There's a lot of talk of starting over in a foreign country. "Do you remember Susan?" a friend asked the other day. "She's in China. She got her life down to four suitcases."

These people are not collectors; hence the disposability of twenty years' accumulation of household goods. A Regency sideboard might have provided some ballast. The absence of anything old or cherished is, I think, a symptom of financial naivety. In all my years in New York, I have few memories of anyone saving for something special. It's sort of pointless if you're twenty-eight and making a hundred thousand a year.

It's hard to survive in that world, if you're an antiques dealer. Possibly things will improve. In any case, I don't see how they can get much worse.

Collecting

What Type of Collector Are You?

AntiqueWeek, August 13, 2007

Any group can be divided, according to this or that trait. Among antique collectors one division is between the directed and the serendipitous.

In the first group are those who frequent the best dealers and buy only what is in good condition and of sound provenance. This style of collecting is a little like paying down your mortgage or saving for retirement. Financial prudence might make you rich, but you won't get your name in the newspaper. Prudence might seem like a curious recommendation from someone who makes a living writing about antiques, but I've always believed that if I were to collect antiques, this is how I would go about it.

Then there are the serendipitous collectors. They go here and there—

everywhere, in fact, except to the conventional venues. That's the giveaway: the belief that the most promising place to look is also the least expected. Skip the vetted antiques show and head straight for the drabbest street vendor you can find. Occasionally, this approach yields a spectacular success, and it is the unexpectedness of the discovery that gets emphasized in the press.

I once arranged to go book hunting with a friend who was optimistic about these accidental finds. We were in a region rich in antiquarian booksellers, but we visited only one in twelve hours on the road. The rest of the time was spent at yard sales. These were not the pickings-rich events organized by your local block association, but unkempt lawns littered with soiled aprons and rusty tools. They were hardly the market for, say, Victorian travel memoirs. We stopped at them all, one by one, on that long Saturday. Somehow my friend, an otherwise shrewd person, believed that our time would be better spent sorting through junk than visiting the first-rate dealers. "This might be it," he would say hopefully, slowing down the car.

I always assumed that this style of collecting was a recent development, one that was influenced by the popularity of eBay and *Antiques Roadshow*. To my surprise, collector's serendipity dates back many years. One of its most persuasive proponents was the nineteenth-century art critic Clarence Cook. His decorating treatise, *The House Beautiful* (1881), is still in print. If you're partial to the aesthetic movement, with its emphasis on art for art's sake, this is the book to read. The colloquial style and illustrations evoke a world of Japanese porcelain and delft-tiled fireplaces.

Cook was writing during the golden age of American collecting. A hard-up man of letters, he believed in the esoteric odds and ends that are the pride of the modest collector. The industrialists—those coarse founders of glue and varnish fortunes—could buy by the gross. But the refined man, Cook argued, was happiest with a chance assemblage of eclectic provenance. His descriptions are often mere lists of these small finds: "Here is the bit of Japanese bronze, or the Satsuma cup, or the Etruscan vase, or the Roman lamp." The noticing connoisseur, during his rambles, might also pick up "a bubble bottle of old Roman glass in the ruined palace of the Caesars." That the bottle might be last year's picnic trash does not, significantly, occur to Cook.

At a distance of more than a century, we can see just how nutty some of Cook's advice was. Take his discussion of early American furniture. In New England, he writes, colonial furniture had passed from fashion, and many of the best pieces had been taken outside and converted into henhouses. "It is surprising to learn to what strange uses things may have come at last," he says. "The back country is scoured by young people in chaises on the trail of old sideboards." I have no idea how accurate Cook's claims were—did the Americana market ever fall that low?—but he makes it all sound so exciting. Instead of giving your money to a stodgy dealer, it was so much more free spirited to rummage around Farmer Brown's chicken coop. If you're caught, just explain that you're looking for a highboy.

I suppose you can gauge Cook's collecting acumen by the one antique he mentions owning. It is a dining table, which he finds "in a certain garret" and buys for practically nothing. Cook cannot believe his luck. It is a little rundown ("one leaf had fallen from its hinges"), but he marvels at what he calls his "good fortune." He shows it to a "friend" who tells him that the table is worth "a great deal more, even as wood, than I had paid for it." Verily, he writes, "those who seek such things are continually finding them."

Sometimes, I acknowledge, those finds are worth big money. For my tastes, though, I prefer to consult the show calendar.

It Doesn't Have to Be the Next Big Thing

***AntiqueWeek*, December 17, 2007**

The press came, as they always do, to the ocean liner sale to see how high prices for *Titanic* relics could go. At Christie's, the back of the room was crowded with cameramen and the seats were filled with bidders and curiosity seekers. Largely forgotten in the enthusiasm for the ghoulish detritus of the famous shipwreck were the postwar lots. Perhaps it's just a matter of time before collectors turn their attention to the midcentury tables and chairs from the *Michelangelo* and *Liberté*.

Predicting the next big thing is what reporters do. Chippendale might have a good run, but after a while, everyone's looking ahead to Regency. And if coverage of that is too saturated, there will be an attempt to steer collectors to something more specialized—say, William IV furniture.

It's just a matter of time, they say, before that long neglected field takes off. There is often a financial angle to these stories. Sometimes it is implied and sometimes it is stated outright, but the message is the same: buy now before prices rise. Readers are left with the impression that they barely have time to put on clean socks and grab their wallet before being shut out forever from all the great deals.

I have often thought that the financial argument for collecting is backwards. Antiques are fun because they are an affordable hobby—and likely to stay that way. After all, no one wants to get all involved in something only to have to drop out a few years later because the expense is too great.

Many auctions are characterized by four or five star lots, dozens of smaller ones that just clear the reserve, and dozens more that are bought in. Successful sales can have short pricelists. It's a little like those mutual fund reports you get from Fidelity. Even in a good year, most of the growth seems to be driven by a handful of companies. But unlike an underperforming stock, do you really want to dump that Victorian punch bowl? It cost only a hundred dollars, which means you have enough left over for a ladle.

As a bibliophile, I happily report that prices are stagnant at the low end of the market. My favorite book fair takes place in February. It's a small event—the venue is a rundown elementary school—that attracts the same bunch of regional dealers, year in, year out. With the ABAA fair two months away, the big collectors can't be bothered. But if you have fifty bucks to spare this is the place to stock up on art nouveau bindings, old children's books, and World War II propaganda.

In the fifteen years I've been attending, the prices have hardly budged. It used to be pretty empty, with a few dozen asocial types sorting through old volumes. Sometime in the late 1990s, they hired a decent publicist. "Here's the end of a good thing," I thought. But no, not at all. There were more people, enticed by the press, but not more buyers.

After years of buying and reselling and buying some more, I would estimate my library is worth at most two thousand dollars. Visitors often disagree with this appraisal. "Surely, these nice old books are worth more," they say. My answer: "Not if I can afford them." I find that usually brings the discussion to a close. The funny thing is that my enjoyment would not be one jot greater, if it turned out that they really were worth something.

In a similar spirit, I once asked a scholarly collector how the market for his field had changed. I was thinking that his three books and many lectures might have increased demand. Nothing had changed, he reported. His esoteric niche of Victorian ceramics was as unfashionable as ever, which meant he was still picking up nice things for less than five thousand dollars.

Here's another anecdote: a dealer in Victorian painting told me about two artists, whose works twenty years ago were selling in the range of eight to ten thousand dollars. Today one artist can be had for twenty thousand dollars, while the other has been catapulted into the hundred-thousand-dollar club.

So which was the better investment? There isn't any doubt from a cold-cash point of view. But the more expensive artist is now out of reach to all but rich collectors. The other can still be picked up by a middle-class connoisseur. Some enterprising person could build a small collection of the artist's work by trawling regional salerooms and arriving early at shows. The pursuit conjures up stimulating weekends meeting with favorite dealers and befriending rival buyers.

Such pleasures are available to all collectors—and that's a point that needs to be emphasized.

Young People Are Having '80s Parties

AntiqueWeek, April 20, 2009

Recently a young coworker mentioned that he hosted a 1980s party. "We ate pasta alfredo and watched *Blue Velvet,*" he said. The idea is not as original as he seemed to think. You hear more and more about these 1980s parties being organized by hip millenials. The girls wear leggings and tease their hair into a big frizzy mess. I'm not sure what the boys wear. The point seems to be a jokey takeoff of the decade's parochialism and pretentiousness. It's startling to think that the years of one's adolescence have been claimed for ironic reenactment.

I've been thinking a lot about the 1980s. I work for an online vendor of estate antiques in Brooklyn. We sell a little of everything. Our inventory is not exactly museum quality but we offer a nice range of silver, porcelain, and glass.

Every week I visit the Upper East Side dealer who supplies us with our stock. He's been cleaning out apartments for fifty years. He passes on not only the Victorian tureens and art deco letter openers but the newish stuff, a category made up largely of unused wedding gifts. While the Tiffany candlesticks and Lalique vases tend to linger in our eBay store, the china is a fast sell. Especially popular are the dishes with colorful birds and flowers on black ground—very crisp and very 1980s.

It is the antiques, however, that remind me most of that decade: vermeil fish knives, little porcelain boxes, and papier-mâché screens—all the superfluous gewgaws that signaled the rediscovery of luxury are crammed in there.

The dealer has entered the hoarding phase of his career, so finding new inventory resembles an excavation. The silver is kept in old brown grocery bags and the showcases of Meissen are hidden behind large portraits. Most everything else is piled pellmell; that too evokes the zealous acquisitiveness of the 1980s. His indifference to modern design is another marker. Teasing things out of him can be a challenge, but while he is retentive of the Sèvres cachepots, he lets go without protest of a midcentury tea service.

There were many influences on home decoration, but it is the English influence that I remember most vividly. Beginning in 1981, when Prince Charles married Lady Diana Spencer, the 1980s were characterized by an enthusiasm for all things English. In 1982, there was *Brideshead Revisited,* the miniseries that was filmed at Castle Howard in Yorkshire. And three years after that, the blockbuster exhibition *The Treasures Houses of Britain* opened at the National Gallery of Art. For connoisseurs of historic interiors the pickings were rich.

Anglophilia is one of those fashions where the superficial flourishes side by side with the serious. In France, in the 1780s, the English taste reflected the desire for political freedom and reform on the eve of revolution. It was, at the same time, the moment when the mahogany dining table came into fashion in France.

The 1980s, likewise, were a time of danger and anxiety. Angus Trumble, a curator at the Yale Center for British Art, is one of the people I spoke to about those days. "The Soviet Union was breathing down the neck of Western Europe," he says. A resurgent Great Britain, under the leadership of Prime Minister Margaret Thatcher, gave hope to the West. The new opulence also coincided with fierce policy debates about the role of government in helping the poor. "People forget how bitter those divisions were," he says.

Not that the decorator picking out lampshades was necessarily thinking about any of these things. But what must have been obvious, even to the sporadic shopper, was the lavishness of furnishings and decoration.

Sharon McCormick, an interior designer in Durham, Connecticut, remembers the style well. Back then, she had just finished her MBA and was working as a CPA. Socially, she ran with other young professionals, who aspired to good jobs and nice homes. "This is when life started getting really busy," she remembers. Many women sought to combine a career with the responsibilities of motherhood and homemaking. While there was more running around, there was also, thanks to the second income, more money for decorating.

Their career choices may have been groundbreaking, but their tastes tended to be traditional. The predominant style was inspired by the English country house. The models were not only Castle Howard but Chatsworth and Badminton, historic stately homes that were featured in magazines, like *Architectural Digest.*

The American version of manorial chic was fussier, brighter, and more cheerful than the real thing. Another trait: the density of ornament. Not since the nineteenth century have rooms been decorated with such a quantity of patterns. The sofa alone, crowded with chintz cushions, might count a half dozen patterns.

Every space was filled. Walls were papered, stenciled, and tiled. Window curtains, at the start of the decade, were unobtrusive panels that ensured privacy and warmth. They metastasized into cascading folds of silk held in place with tasseled tiebacks.

For the adventurous—and masochistic—there were the DIY decorating manuals that were published by Laura Ashley and Conran's, two English design firms that were in their heyday. Tenting a room was one of the spare-time projects that could be attempted. "Just think of a theme and choose the fabric that best expresses it," cheerily begins one set of instructions, followed by pages of dense type and diagrams that assume Nobel Prize-caliber spatial-visual skills.

The new way spilled over into the related activity of collecting. The serendipitous pace of accumulation became more concentrated, McCormick recalls. Weekends were spent, in her words, "on the hunt" in auction houses and antiques stores. The competition was strong for Staffordshire figurines and other English curios that were displayed en masse in the home. "They had to be all out together," she testifies. "Every single tabletop was covered with books and figurines." And the table, most likely, was covered with a short square cloth draped over a ruffled floor-length one.

The style was a boon for the antiques trade. By the 1990s, the look was hopelessly out of date. Maintenance was onerous. The dusting alone took hours. Inevitably, there was a reaction in the form of plain white dishes and boxy taupe sofas. I feel nostalgic because I make my living selling antiques, but I wouldn't want to live that way.

Disappearance of Long Island Estate Auctions

AntiqueWeek, June 18, 2012

The Long Island estate sale was once a fixture of the New York art market. Sometimes it was on-site in Oyster Bay or Glen Cove, but more often the Parke-Bernet people would pack everything up and take it back to their Madison Avenue saleroom. "Property from a Long Island estate" was a cliché of big city auctions.

There is no need to exaggerate the importance of these long ago sales. The catalogs with their flimsy paper covers and cursory descriptions make clear that many people were selling Grandma's things: rosewood whatnots, tufted settees, and moldy specimens of the taxidermist's art. Has anything ever seemed more old fashioned than

Victoriana in the 1930s and 1940s? But then there was the really old stuff, like the colonial tankard, a regimental gift to the consignor's great-great-grandfather. To think it was coming on the market after all those years in the Dutch cupboard.

Quite a lot has changed since then. For one, only a few Long Island estates are left.

In 2007, one of the last went on the block. Margaret Phipps Boegner had an impeccable Gilded Age pedigree. Her paternal grandfather was a friend and associate of Andrew Carnegie, while her mother's family founded a shipping firm. She grew up in Old Westbury, in an English redbrick manor. When Mrs. Boegner was in her fifties, the estate was opened to the public as Old Westbury Gardens. She moved next door to a smaller house, taking with her many of the furnishings from her childhood home.

Her heirs sold the family silver (mostly Georgian) not to mention the Chippendale chairs, diamond tiaras, and Victorian landscapes at South Bay Auctions in East Moriches.

An estate sale—and I mean estate in the sense of historic property, not as a euphemism for dead consignor—can be the highlight of the auction season. But every time an estate is sold, there is one less that can be sold in the future. And despite all the money that was flying around, it doesn't look like they're being replaced. The single-owner sale is the future of the trade. Some rich and energetic person assembles a hundred first-rate pieces of arts & crafts furniture. He "grows" the collection (as they say in the financial press) for ten or twenty years, before selling it off, out of boredom or on the advice of his accountant.

Nostalgia is understandable in a market dominated by these temporary assemblages of top-tier objects. In a room filled with masterpieces, even the specialist can feel overpowered and pine for the haphazard and accretive charm of the old family place.

Many years ago in France, I stayed with some friends at their country house. The house, which had been in the family for centuries, symbolized a geographic stability practically unthinkable to an American. "We've had this a while" was a statement that could refer to twenty years ago or before the French Revolution.

Even events from the last forty or fifty years seemed lost in a primeval past. I was lodged in the new wing (late Louis XIV), in the *chambre des Anglaises*. The room took its name from a visit made by some English girls a half century before. It was the storeroom for anything British, including dozens of Agatha Christie's novels that someone had accumulated in the 1960s. But just as no one could remember very much about the English girls, so too was uncertain the identity of the mystery fan who assembled the library. Perhaps it was one of the elderly men I saw at dinner who, in his days as a young son-in-law, used the room as a hideaway from the importunities of his wife's family.

The one good piece—a secretary that was, according to family tradition, a gift from Marie-Antoinette—had been sold. The dusty patch of parquet that it had occupied was left empty and surrounded by tables, chairs, and chests crammed with old letters. At one point my hosts fished out the manicure set that had belonged to the American lady who had married somebody's uncle after the war (which war?). She died alone and unexpectedly, many years ago, but they still had her things.

They had everybody's things. There was nothing really important. It was the jumbled detritus of all those lives that was poignant—and very different from all the modern houses decorated to suggest jumbled detritus.

It's a distinction I have occasion to make when I write for the house and garden press. Many years ago, I wrote a feature about a decorator, who talked his clients into the eclectic look: an African mask above a rococo table next to a Queen Anne candle stand. The results, judging by his apartment, were awful. "Not a slave to historical precision" was, I recall, how I euphemistically summed up the look.

It was not a lively, chatty interview. He lolled on the sofa while I was parked on a spindly ballroom chair. We were separated by acres of sisal carpeting. Here is one telltale exchange: "I always tell clients to surround themselves with things that have meaning. Display family things, even if they're not stylish," he declared with more force than originality. Inevitably, I followed up: "What are the things that mean the most to you?" He looked around the room. He looked around again. Then he said, "I keep a lot of things in storage. I don't have them out at the moment."

Some days he was in a sporting prints mood. Other days he saw himself as a connoisseur of Asian bronzes. But in the end it was always about his perception of himself. He had many old things but nothing that suggested past lives.

A sense of past lives is what can be found at an estate sale. Let's hope that's what bidders took away from the Phipps auction because there will not be many more like it.

Ikea and the Promises of No Emotional Attachment

***AntiqueWeek*, January 7, 2013**

I used to teach a class on historic interiors. Most lessons were slide lectures, but occasionally I'd organize a visit to the Metropolitan Museum of Art. The decorative arts galleries were a powerful didactic tool: rows of chronologically arranged furnishings that let you trace the history of a style in a few steps. But that's not what my students came to see. The period rooms were their preferred destination. To have a sense of what life was like in eighteenth-century France, they needed the mise en scène of marquetry tables, Sèvres vases, and gilt-white boiserie.

What life was like was only approximately captured by the early museum period rooms. In *Moving Rooms: The Trade in Architectural Salvage* (Yale University Press, 2007), the author John Harris recounts their sometimes composite and fraudulent origins. The modern versions are more accurate, but my students were indifferent to refinements of lighting and installation. The splendor and fantasy were the attraction.

The Met isn't the only place in New York to see period rooms. The Brooklyn Museum and Museum of the City of New York also have them. But for me the most poignant period rooms are at Ikea. In this case period refers not to a time in history but a time in your life—the post-college twenty-something years when you have big dreams and not much money. Everything is possible because nothing has been tried. The intensity is suggested by the dimensions of the Ikea starter apartments. In most parts of the country, a 250 square-foot apartment is proof you have lost life's lottery. Not in New York where home is a rest station to be visited between stretches of absorbing work and lively, witty parties. The milieu is urban bohemia. Hence the wall-mount laptop case above the kitchen table, so you can work on your novel before setting out for the gallery or publishing house.

Well, that's how it should be. Because the Ikea rooms are also an approximate ideal. At that age, your career is years away from offering intellectual stimulation. As for the parties, I remember talk that managed to be both humorless and unserious. Enjoyment (if that's what it's called) was permitted only through a prism of ironic estrangement. Still, I feel a pang of irrational longing when I tour these rooms.

I like Ikea. I spend more time there than is correct for someone who works in the antiques trade. For many years, a trip to Ikea meant taking a shuttle bus to New Jersey. Departure from the Port Authority Terminal was followed by a long drive on big strange roads. But then we got an Ikea of our own. It is located in Red Hook, Brooklyn, in the old naval yard. Where battleships were built to defeat the Axis Powers stands a warehouse filled with made-in-China Scandinavian design. A trip there has a holiday feel. I arrive on an elevated train, which never fails to evoke the amusement park monorail in Seattle, where I grew up.

Probably you're expecting me to comment on the shoddiness of the merchandise. I'll get to that in a minute. First, let me say how many beautiful things there are. My favorites are the glass and ceramics. I should know better, but I rarely leave the store without a six-pack of mugs or tumblers. Also, the paper napkins: bright and pretty squares that enliven the matte grays and greens that Ikea favors.

These things can be had for a derisory price. They're immediately replaceable in case of chips or breaks. Tire of them, and they can be donated without guilt to the Salvation Army. And they are what they say they are. "Ikea of Sweden. Made in China" reads the back stamp. Yup, that's right. No authentication problems here. True, they evoke no family memories or appreciation of century-old craftsmanship. But I don't usually think about those things when I am making my tea. Six in the morning is a little early for elegiac emotions.

Stick to the occasional smalls and Ikea is unobjectionable. It's the furniture that causes problems. Getting it home is a pain, if you don't own a car (a common situation in New York City). Assembly is required, and the finished product never looks quite like it does in the showroom. It doesn't age well nor does it absorb the daily pileups. The designs work only if you have no more possessions than what the wardrobes and cupboards can hold. A stack of books next to a Billy bookcase suggests not an overflowing literary appetite but slovenly housekeeping. And it can be displayed only with other Ikea furniture. Proximity to real furniture emphasizes the flimsy construction and shiny finish.

Obvious points that we know by heart. But it's not enough to point out that the free-spirited Ikea interior involves hassles and inconvenience. After all, the antique interior can be just as complicated. No assembly is required, but there are the burdens of maintenance and durability. There lurks too the hope of owning something valuable. That the least promising objects turn out to be worth the most money is a perception associated, perhaps unfairly, with *Antiques Roadshow*. So the dented silver-plate tray is never taken out of the felt bag. You can't be too careful with precious things. With the appraisal comes disappointment. Antiques can let you down in a way that the flat pack never does.

At least we have history on our side. Our inventory offers a connection with the past. But that's not what people appear to be looking for. Ikea shoppers know the stuff is disposable. They don't expect it to last. That's one reason they're buying it. Heirlooms can be a deadweight. "You will have this for the rest of your life," says the antiques dealer. It's a remark that can induce secret panic. Like a needy friend, that antique will be with you forever. You can never part. It's your duty to care for it—to protect it and clean it and repair it, if necessary. The promise of Ikea is freedom from such responsibility. And very attractive that promise is—even to some of us who know better.

Rural Italian Holiday is a Much Safer Trip Today

AntiqueWeek, June 24, 2013

When you open your mailbox this summer, you're certain to pull out at least one postcard from Italy. It might show the Leaning Tower of Pisa or the Colosseum in Rome, but it is just as likely to show a village in Tuscany. There your correspondent and his family are enjoying two weeks of exotic rusticity. For lodgings, they have rented a house—perhaps a dilapidated manse or renovated barn. Even more improbably, their days are spent hanging out at agriculture fairs and lounging in dingy cafes.

The allure of experiencing rural life overseas is fairly common, thanks to the Internet, which has simplified reservations.

Thus Americans, who would not dream of renting a farmhouse in Nebraska, are vacationing in Italian hamlets too obscure to merit mention in a Victorian Baedeker.

To appreciate the reversal of values represented by this fashion, it is worth considering how things used to be done. Especially instructive are the experiences of the English grand tourists who traveled to Italy during the eighteenth century.

Three hundred years ago, the Italian countryside was a place of hunger, lawlessness, and filth. Conditions were such that today they would very likely be the subject of a State Department advisory.

Our modern bucolic fantasies would have found little resonance among the grand tourists. They did not linger in the country, and their memoirs recount early risings and long days in their haste to reach their destination. Bad roads were one problem; another was brigandage. "In ascending the mountain we met two or three little parties of very ill-looking fellows," wrote one lady, who was made equally nervous by her native coachman.

We are accustomed to thinking of wealth as a guarantee of protection and ease, so that it is difficult to imagine the hardship inherent in travel in earlier centuries. Neither money nor social rank provided nearly as much insulation as they do today in matters of transportation and lodging. In the cities, rich foreigners could enjoy the local cuisine, and their rooms were often, literally, palatial.

But the belief that, if you pay enough money, your journey will be comfortable, even enjoyable, was less developed during the eighteenth century. Rotten food and fetid accommodations were perfectly normal when moving from one city to another.

Eyewitness descriptions of the rural inns are especially grim. Travelers might disagree on the merits of the Sistine Chapel, but their views of these establishments are remarkably uniform. "Gnats, bugs, fleas, and lice" was how Samuel Sharp, a London surgeon, summarized the problem in the 1760s. To escape the vermin it was prudent to pass the night on a table or bench, which was uncomfortable—but surely preferable to the consequences of sleeping beneath the covers. "All the way to Naples we never once crept within the sheets, not daring to encounter the vermin and nastiness of those beds," Sharp reported.

Indeed, the allusions to bedbugs diminish considerably any prurient assumptions about life on the road. When one young lord wrote in his diary, "What a night have I passed," he was referring only to some bug bites "on a very tender part, which I shall forbear mentioning."

To round out this account there should be some mention of the sporadic disposal of waste. In their depiction of the Italian inn, travel memoirs evoke an atmosphere of eye-watering stench.

Nor did the meals make up for the nights of vermin and foul smells. "Now and then we get a little piece of mutton, or veal, and generally speaking, it is the only eatable morsel that falls in our way," wrote Sharp about the dinners that he and his family were served (on dirty dishes, it is perhaps unnecessary to specify). Many travelers, it appears, simply went hungry.

The grand tour had serious social and artistic objectives that compensated for the ghastly travel conditions. "The horrors of an Italian journey" (Sharp's phrase) were endured because travelers wanted to see the finest artifacts of civilization. Classical art was especially important, though visitors also spent many days touring the churches and palaces. These tastes were reflected in their collecting. Roman sculpture and Renaissance paintings were especially prized.

There were battlefields and aqueducts to be seen en route, but the really important sites—the statues and ruins that could not be overlooked—were usually located in or near a city. Back then, travel was urban in character. Going to Italy to stay on a farm would have been considered eccentric not to mention reckless.

Italian cities are today more crowded than ever, with hotels booked full and long lines at the museums. Small wonder that some tourists want to skip it all and head straight for the country.

Still, although rural life has improved since the eighteenth century, hardships remain. So be patient when your friends show you another picture of the village feed store. They endured two weeks of chill rooms and bad television reception—and who knows what was lurking between those damp sheets.

About the Author

Amy Gale lives in New York City, where she catalogs silver and reads French novels. Her writing has been published in *Accent Home & Garden, Antik & Auktion, Antiques & Auction News, Antiques & Collecting, Antiques & Fine Art, Antiques and the Arts Weekly, Antiques Info, AntiqueWeek, Art & Antiques, Art + Auction, @UCSD, Bob Vila Online, Book Source Magazine, Cape Cod & Islands Home, Cape Cod Life, Chicago Tribune, Christian Science Monitor, Classic American Home, Collectables Trader, Dime Novel Roundup, Hartford Courant, Home & Design, New England Antiques Journal, New York Home, Newsday, Quest, Renovation Style, Southern Accents, Studies in the Decorative Arts, Style 1900, Victorian Homes,* and *World of Antiques & Art.*

4938147R00095

Printed in Great Britain
by Amazon.co.uk, Ltd.,
Marston Gate.